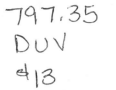

JUN 1992

CAMILLE DUVALL'S

INSTRUCTIONAL
GUIDE TO

**WATER
SKIING**

by

Camille Duvall

with

Nancy Crowell

PHOTOGRAPHS BY TOM KING

A FIRESIDE BOOK
PUBLISHED BY SIMON & SCHUSTER
New York London Toronto Sydney Tokyo Singapore

F

FIRESIDE
Simon & Schuster Building
Rockefeller Center
1230 Avenue of the Americas
New York, New York 10020

Designed by Black Angus Design Group
Manufactured in the United States of America

10 9 8 7 6 5 4 3 2 1

Library of Congress Cataloging in Publication Data
Duvall, Camille.
   [Instructional guide to water skiing]
   Camille Duvall's instructional guide to water skiing/by Camille
Duvall with Nancy Crowell; photographs by Tom King.
      p.   cm.
   "A Fireside book."
   1. Water skiing.   I. Crowell, Nancy.   II. Title.
GV840.S5D88   1992
797.3'5—dc20   92-3657
                                                    CIP

ISBN: 0-671-74640-5

ACKNOWLEDGMENTS

To my husband, Byron, and my son, Alexander—thanks for always being there for me, and for giving me the confidence I need when the going gets tough.

To my father, I'm glad I could fulfill your dream.

To my mother, without your dedication and strength I would not have six world championships to count.

To my brother, Sammy, for your belief in me all these years.

To Chuck Dees, Liz Allen, Rick McCormick, Linda Giddens, Jack Travers, and Sammy Duvall—the best coaches a girl could have.

To Jack and Bobby, who have pulled me to more pro slalom titles than anyone.

Special thanks to my sponsors—O'Brien Skis, Danskin, and Killer Loop Sunglasses—without their financial support over the years things would have been really tough.

And special thanks to Marco Bettosini, Dale St. John, Ron Scarpa, Margie Gerding, Jim Piatt, Denny Kidder and Ellen Leventhal.

CONTENTS

FOREWORD

What would you like to know about water skiing? Maybe you are fascinated by the people and their climb to success. Perhaps you'd like to know how to begin so that you might compete with the world's elite ski masters, or just blow away all your friends on the lake. For all of this and more, you have the right book, written by the most qualified ski champion, Camille Duvall.

I met Camille at The Masters Water Ski Tournament at Calloway Gardens, Georgia in 1985. Of all the women who were competing, Camille showed the greatest combination of technique, athletic ability, and aggressive desire to become a champion. Camille understands how to achieve this success and is always articulate in communicating these ideas. I believe that natural talent, as great and wonderful as it is, will always come in second place when competing with discipline, knowledge and hard work. To be a champion in this sport, you have to pull it all together.

Camille, by her talent and charm, motivated me to take up the sport. I am living proof that if you don't want to become a champion skier, then you can still learn how to have fun from Camille's book. I've always needed help on the best way to fall after trying to jump over the wake.

Camille comes from a family of skiers who have enjoyed this growing sport on all levels. The fact that Camille is now sharing her experience and knowledge with us is a gift for skiing enthusiasts at every stage.

As a matter of fact, Camille sent me a competition ski, with a few hints as to how it should be used. Not only did I have great fun skiing on it, I bought a boat to make sure that I could ski whenever I had the time. My friends and family have enjoyed some priceless moments on lakes and rivers around the country.

I know that you will enjoy this book and all that Camille Duvall has to offer as America's "Queen of Water Skiing."

—Lynn Swann
January 1992

INTRODUCTION

I have been water skiing since I was four years old. Although my introduction to the sport was inauspicious at best (more on that later), I can truly say that since the very beginning, this sport has brought me considerable pleasure and personal satisfaction. I have grown to love it more and more, and I hope by introducing you to the sport, and offering some short cuts and tips, you, too, will share my enthusiasm and perhaps even adopt the sport as your own favorite water sport. Even to this day, I find water skiing exhilarating.

In fact, one of the most memorable days of my life centers on water skiing. It was the day I won my fifth world professional slalom championship on the Coors Light Tour, in 1988. Just six weeks before the start of the 1988 season I had my shoulder operated on. It was a frightening prospect to face the season with so little time to prepare, but I had four world professional slalom championships behind me and was determined to keep on winning.

At the first event of the season I came in a disappointing fourth place. All the other women were skiing well, and I knew I would have to get in shape quickly if I wanted to defend my title. (The world professional championship on the Coors Light Tour is based on cumulative tournaments, so the entire season is very important.) In the past, most of my championships had required my beating long-time rival, Deena Mapple. She was generally stronger in jumping, I in slalom, and it seemed every tournament came down to the two of us. But by 1988 there were half a dozen other strong contenders in the field, and the days of Deena and I dominating water skiing were rapidly coming to a close.

That summer was a blur of long, hard weekends for me. I skied inconsistently as I tried to get back to full strength. Some weekends I was hot in competition, other weekends went to other victors. In the end, it all came down to the final tournament of the season in Wichita, Kansas to determine who would win the world professional championship. Going in to the tournament there was a three-way tie for the title between Jennifer Leachman, Canadian Susi Graham, and me. Complicating matters was the fact that Susi Graham was my best friend. It's never easy to compete against a good friend.

The tension was high among us as we started the first round. Jennifer became a victim of her own nerves, as she missed the entrance gates on her first pass and therefore disqualified herself. Susi was knocked out in the semifinals, but I still had to win the tournament in order to win the title. With Susi and Jennifer knocked out of it, I found myself in the semifinals once again face to face with my old nemesis—Deena Mapple.

The skiing conditions were horrible. It was windy and there was lots of backwash through the course. Even the guys were having a tough time of it. But I knew Deena was tough, so I had to concentrate. I went first and managed to ski around three buoys at the 40′ rope length. She could only manage two buoys at the same length. That put me in the finals against world amateur slalom champion Kim Laskoff.

Kim can be inconsistent. One never knows if she's going to be dead on, or not make it at all. She skied first, and as I sat in the water at the other end of the slalom course waiting for her to finish her run, I was more nervous than I'd ever been.

Kim skied great. Maybe the best she had skied all year—certainly the best anyone had done in these conditions. She ran three and a half buoys at the 40′ rope length. I thought at first she was going to get all six buoys, but even when she made three and a half I knew I had my work cut out for me.

Suddenly my nervousness subsided as I realized that I had trained all my life for this very moment. I focused on exactly what I needed to do to win the tournament (and my fifth world title): get around that fourth buoy. I focused so intensely on that one goal that when I made it, I fell attempting to round the fifth buoy. When I came up from under the water all my emotions poured out of me in a torrent of tears. I don't know if I could have finished the entire run—it's possible. All I know is that I had set my sights on a goal and had achieved it.

I had become engaged a few months earlier, and my fiance Byron had supported me 100 percent through my surgery and the long, hard months on the tour. Needless to say, he was elated, and I even felt I had done it as much for him as for myself. My brother Sammy, also a world overall champion, was just as proud and couldn't restrain himself as he watched and did color commentary for ESPN. It was one of the most thrilling moments of my life.

I'd like you to experience moments like that with your water skiing. Even if you don't win a world championship you can still get the same thrill from the sport I've enjoyed all my life. For you, the moment might be the first time you get up on a slalom ski. Or it might be the first time you make it all the way through the course. Whatever level skier you are, this book will share with you my experiences and tips from over twenty-five years in this sport. It will help you avoid some of the pitfalls I've faced, and will cover everything from the easiest way to install a slalom course, to how to size your bindings, to how to get the most out of watching a professional event on television.

Water skiing has a long and proud history. From Ralph Samuelson's first brave attempts in 1922, the sport has had dozens of notable greats, each of whom has advanced it another notch. I am thankful for skiers such as Liz Allen, Wayne Grimditch, Mike Suyderhoud, Jimmy "the Flea" Jackson, Alfredo Mendoza, Willa McGuire Cook, Dick Pope and Barbara Cooper Clack, and Ricky McCormick, for without them pushing the limits of possibilities I would surely not enjoy earning my living today as a full-time professional water skier. With this book, I hope to encourage and teach a new generation of skiers who some day may join these greats in the Water Ski Hall of Fame.

As you begin this book, let me offer just one bit of advice. The key to becoming great in this sport or any other is to have fun. If it's not fun for you, you won't want to do it. Twenty-six years since I first learned, I still have fun water skiing. I hope you will, too.

ONE

ESSENTIAL EQUIPMENT

EVERY WATER SKIER DREAMS of a warm, sunny day; a ski boat with a skilled driver at the wheel; and a glass-calm lake no one else has discovered. Makes your heart beat a little faster just thinking about it, doesn't it?

New boat owners often feel the same way when they antici-pate getting out on the water for the first time. They're so excited about the new boat that reason flies out the window, and they purchase the first pair of skis a dealer shows them, just so they will have *something* to use when they get to the water.

I've learned from experience as both a competitive skier and a teacher that good equipment is the key to great skiing, so hold off on that impulse buy. If you follow my recommendations, you'll save both money and frustration, and the equipment you buy will last through many seasons of sunny days and calm waters.

Shredding glass is every skier's dream.

BARE NECESSITIES—PFDs

Your boat dealer will no doubt inform you that the law re-quires you to have Coast Guard–approved PFDs (personal flotation devices) for each person on board. But don't just grab the least expensive life jackets you can find and toss them in the boat. The Coast Guard approves a variety of PFDs; as a skier, you have several options to consider.

Most skiers favor the Type III PFD. (Most PFDs will have the Coast Guard Type number on a label, usually attached to the inside of the jacket; Types represent different category specifications for approved PFDs.) Here are a few things you should look for in a jacket to be used for skiing.

First, the jacket should close by buckles, a front zipper, or both, and it should close completely. (Think about it—can you imagine how it would feel to take a bad fall in a jacket where the buckles were right next to your chest? Ouch!) Second, the armholes should be large enough for ample freedom of movement. My personal preference is for jackets that are long enough to cover the vital organs. In other words, they cover your navel, usually down to or below your hip bones. The jacket should not be so large that, when you're in the water, it floats above your ears. You can test this on dry land by making sure you've got a jacket that fits snugly when buckled.

Life jackets are made of several different kinds of material. As a professional skier, I use one made of neoprene (wetsuit material), but I recommend a jacket with more flotation for recreational skiers. I don't recommend the shiny, soft vinyl jackets that appear to come out of a mold—they can stick to your skin and they don't last as long. That leaves jackets covered with nylon as the best choice. Whatever you choose, do not buy life jackets with extra neckpieces if you plan to use them for skiing. They are bulky and uncomfortable. And the old-fashioned "ski belts" are unsafe and strictly taboo. They're not approved PFDs.

One last note about PFDs. Most ski companies make PFDs to match their skis, so if you like a professional, color-coordinated look, consider this possibility.

TOWROPES

Once you've selected jackets for everyone in the family, and a spare or two for guests, you're ready to grab a rope and go, right? Well, yes and no. Although a skiing towrope may seem

(clockwise from bottom) Old-fashioned ski belts are taboo because they aren't Coast Guard–approved PFDs. A ski vest that has a collar will restrict movement. Vinyl vests tend to break down in sunlight. Nylon-covered or neoprene vests are ideal for skiers, especially when they are designed, as these are, specifically for skiing —with extra-large armholes and a snug fit.

like a simple item to buy, beware. There's more to it than you might think.

A standard towline is 70 feet long with a 5-foot handle bridle, making the entire length 75 feet. Towlines that are one continuous length of rope, with no loops for adjustments, are known as jump lines. Those that have multiple loops at specific line lengths are slalom lines; they can be progressively shortened for slalom competition. Don't dismiss the possibility of purchasing the slalom line. As you'll learn, it may be the ideal choice for you.

Towlines are available in three different materials. The least expensive type is an eight-strand monofilament line. These can be very stretchy, but even worse, they won't last. They don't have ultraviolet inhibitors to keep them from breaking down in the sun. Twelve-strand polypropylene ropes, on the other hand, are specially designed to take the kind of pull a skier can put on a rope. These are what professional skiers use, some of whom can exert up to 1,200 pounds per square inch of force when they're skiing hard. Polypropylene ropes have a more consistent pull than monofilament; they have ultraviolet inhibitors to make them more durable, and they float.

There is also a rope made with a Kevlar core for dead pull, or no stretch. This is a specialty rope designed for trick skiing and barefoot skiing, and it is very expensive. You won't need it when you're starting out.

Let's return to the difference between the one-piece jump line and the seven-loop or more slalom line. Slalom skiers use the loops to shorten the length of the rope each time they pass through the course successfully. This adds to the challenge of slalom by forcing the skier to stretch and lean over more in order to ski wide enough to continue around the buoys. But trickers and kneeboarders also use these ropes because a shorter rope brings them closer to the boat where the wakes are closer to-gether, giving them greater opportunities to try new tricks. For riding in inner-tube type water toys, if you want to be bounced around and over the wakes—this is the rope to choose. So, if you'll be pulling any recreational kneeboarders or tubers, or if someone in your family is interested in learning to trick ski, look for the seven-loop slalom line.

The handle that is attached to the line is just as important as the line itself. Handles usually come already attached to the lines, but you can always buy one separately and put it on your line. Although double handles are still made, the single handle is safer and easier to use as there is less chance of becoming tangled in the rope handles and if you intend to learn one-handle slalom turns a single handle is a must. They are generally made of aluminum tubing that is filled with wood to prevent bending and covered with some type of soft grip material. Probably the most popular grip material is smooth rubber, which feels tacky when used with ski gloves.

Handles come in three shapes: round, triangular, and oval. Most professionals choose round. You should choose whatever feels best in your hand. Keep in mind that if children will be using it, the handle should be small enough for their grip, too. (This is akin to choosing a tennis racket for your whole family—there will be some trade-off.) Most pro skiers have their own personal handle that they take to tournaments (the actual seventy-foot line is considered tournament equipment and each skier must use the same one in the interest of fair competition) because through consistent use it begins to conform to the shape of their hands.

Remember to purchase several towlines and a few extra PFDs. It's often fun to pull two or more skiers at once, and that extra line will come in handy when you do the inevitable and cut your own line with the propeller.

Learn how to coil your rope and tie it after skiing. This not only prevents knots but helps the rope last longer.

Coiling the rope properly after skiing prevents knots and makes the rope last longer.

SKIS—THE BIG DECISION

COMBOS FIRST

Now that you've seen there's more to buying life jackets and towlines than you'd ever imagined, you're probably prepared to be overwhelmed by the choice of skis on the market. Don't be. There are some basic rules to follow that will help you make the right choice.

The best starting point for a family new to skiing is a good pair of combination skis. Combos, as they're called, are two nearly identical skis designed to be easy to ski on. They are wide in the front and taper slightly to the tail; the large surface area at the front of the skis makes them stable and easy to get up on. They should have adjustable bindings, and one ski should have a rear toe binding so that when you are proficient enough you can use it as a starter slalom ski. Combos range from 64 inches to 67 inches in length and their bottoms can be flat, concave, or have a slight tunnel down the middle. Like tennis rackets and snow skis, they are no longer made of wood but of high-tech composites. The best ones are manufactured by the compression-molding process. Less expensive, and less durable, are those that are reaction-injection molded (RIM).

You can buy combination skis in any price range. I recommend purchasing the very best pair you can afford. Even if you progress quickly to slalom skiing, combos last a long time and will always be needed for teaching friends and family members. Look for compression-molded skis with a slight tunnel shape on the bottom. These will be at the higher end of the price range but are more stable than flat skis. The bindings on the more expensive skis are made of a higher quality rubber and offer more support, making it easier for beginning skiers to control the skis. Choose the 67-inch length—it works best for the widest variety of skiers.

MOVING UP—SLALOM SKIS

Once you've mastered skiing on one ski and are proficient at crossing wakes in both directions, you are ready to invest in your first official slalom ski—a higher performance ski. But don't go straight from combos to a super high performance ski. The top competition skis are generally narrower in the front and are therefore much more difficult to get up on. They also have a little more drag, which will tire you more quickly. Finally, they are much more expensive, and as a beginner, you simply won't be using the technology you're paying for!

A good salesperson will help you determine the type of ski you need based on several factors, including your level of proficiency, the type of skiing you do (at slow speeds; on big, rough lakes, rivers, or small, calm lakes; freestyling, or slalom skiing), your physical size and strength, and the amount of money you want to spend. In addition, there are a variety of features to consider, including the perimeter shape of the ski, length, the bevel shapes (edges), bottom shape, fin shape, and bindings.

For new slalom skiers, an intermediate-level ski is the best choice. You can pick out an intermediate ski yourself by noting that its nose is wider and squarer than that of a competition ski but not as wide as a combo ski. Intermediate-level slalom skis have a medium taper from the forebody to the tail, and the bottom design can be a tunnel, concave, or a combination of both. They will be a little stiffer than a combo when you try to bend them, and their side bevels have more defined facets, making them more performance-oriented than combos.

The bindings on slalom skis can be adjustable or fixed. If the binding is fixed it will be individually fitted for you; if adjustable, other people can use it. Bindings might have high wraps or double-high wraps—wide straps of rubber material that crisscross the ankle for extra stability.

Intermediate skis are available in any length, from a kid's ski

of 60 inches up to a large adult's ski of 72 inches. Like combos, intermediate skis can be either RIM or compression molded.

Don't choose a ski by its color or graphics. To get the right ski for you, ask a salesperson for help; your skiing ability, your weight and the length of the ski are important considerations.

There are several levels of intermediate skis. Base your selection on how far you want to go with your skiing—not everyone wants to progress to the slalom course and compete in tournaments. Also consider locale. Longer skis are better for the rough water often found on large lakes. Shorter skis will turn sharper and work better on small, calm lakes. So consider where you'll be skiing and what your goals are, and share this information with your salesperson.

Advanced skis are designed for many different skiing styles and preferences. While they can vary in shape, they are generally narrow on the front tip to help with deceleration and turning. (If the ski is narrow in the front, it will go deeper into the water when a skier initiates a turn, thus slowing the ski more. This is discussed in later chapters.)

Advanced skis have different-shaped bevels, which affect the way the ski actually initiates the turn. If the bevel is rounded, the water flows by the ski a little more easily and the ski sinks deeper. As you turn the ski you will likely be conscious of the ski rolling over on its edge very easily.

With a ski that has sharp-edged bevels, the flow of water is more defined, and so it is harder to initiate the turn but once on

A comparison of the shapes of these skis and the types of bindings: the intermediate ski is narrower on the front and tail; the advanced ski is narrower still, with plenty of rocker; and the beginner ski is wide and flat, with an adjustable binding.

its edge the ski actually falls noticeably from bevel to bevel as it turns. This type of ski will actually feel as if it is pivoting. (To get a clearer picture of bevel shapes, see the list of factors that affect ski performance later in this chapter.)

Some skis offer a combination of these features at different points along the edge. In this way the skis can accommodate different skiing styles. By the time you can ski well enough to need one of these skis, you will have a good idea what your style is.

In general, the size of the ski is based on one's height and weight. Most ski companies print a height and weight chart to aid customers in choosing the right ski. This is usually a pretty good indicator, because the skis have been designed to meet these specifications. For example, an average-size woman of 5 feet 5 inches weighing 118 pounds could use a ski that is 65 inches long or less, depending on her skill level, but nothing under 60 inches. A man, 6 feet tall and weighing 180 pounds would use a 66-inch ski or longer. A smaller man may want a shorter ski, and a bigger woman may want a longer ski. Most pro women use a 65-inch ski—I happen to use a 66.

RECOMMENDED SKI LENGTHS

Weight (lbs.)	Ski Length (inches)
under 140	64
140–175	66
over 175	67 or 68

SPACE-AGE MATERIALS

Today, most manufacturers have entered the "space age," and skis are made out of fiberglass with some kind of interior strengthening fiber—graphite, Kevlar, or ceramic composite. The amount and type of fibers used and their placement affect the stiffness of the ski. This is an important performance factor when you're running the slalom course because the stiffer the ski, the faster the ski. It's safe to say, however, that stiffness shouldn't be a major priority for intermediate, recreational slalom skiers.

As I mentioned before, skis can be either RIM or compression-molded. Compression molding is a much more labor-intensive method of building skis. The manufacturer takes a foam core cut in the shape of the ski. This core is then wrapped with several layers of fiberglass, applied so that the weave coverage is multidirectional. Sandwiched in between the fiberglass are the strengthening fibers (graphite, Kevlar, etc.) in varying combinations and positions within the ski to control stiffness and rocker or the overall bend from tip to tail. Once it's all assembled, the wrapped core is soaked in epoxy resin. Then the ski is dropped into a stainless-steel mold and the top and bottom are pressed onto it. This whole sandwich is then heat pressed.

CROSS SECTION OF SKI

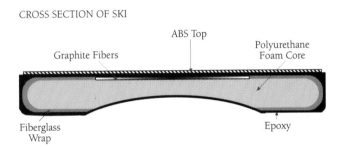

Graphite Fibers
ABS Top
Polyurethane Foam Core
Fiberglass Wrap
Epoxy

Cross-section of a ski
Graphite fibers
ABS top
Polyurethane foam core
Fiberglass wrap
Epoxy

The molds for these skis are very expensive because each is individually handmade by skilled craftsmen. Obviously, there must be a different mold for each ski a company manufactures.

RIM skis, on the other hand, are composed of a polyurethane body with an integral skin (like a sausage casing), steel or fiberglass rods running lengthwise inside the foam body, and a laminate or aluminum top. The ski is made by placing the rods and top in a mold and injecting material through a port in the tail end—much like filling a doughnut with jelly.

Advanced skis are all compression-molded. If you're looking at a RIM ski that is described as advanced, you don't want it; it simply won't be stiff or durable enough.

Ski manufacturers vary the perimeter shape (silhouette) of their skis, the bottom design, the side cuts (or bevels), the rocker (the bend from tip to tail), the flex (the amount of stiffness), and the fin shape to match specific styles of skiing. Keep in mind that all of these factors work in concert to make a ski ride a certain way.

SIX FACTORS THAT AFFECT SKI PERFORMANCE

BOTTOM DESIGN

1. BOTTOM DESIGN
- Narrow tunnels are more stable and track better
- Rails provide lift and stability
- Wide concaves sit deeper, change edges with less effort, and feel less stable on the water
- Shallow concaves cause the ski to ride higher on the water, making for easier turns
- Fan-shaped, or nonconstant concaves have a larger surface area in the tunnel and thus create more suction

BEVELS

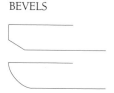

2. BEVELS
- Sharp bevels provide lift for the ski, keeping the ski fast and dry—no spray
- A round bevel allows the ski to roll from edge to edge more easily
- The larger the bevel, the slower the ski will be due to drag, but it will be more stable than one with a small bevel
- The smaller the bevel, the higher the ski will ride
- Two to three bevel shapes running the length of the ski is not uncommon; the different types are used on different portions of the ski

PERIMETER SHAPE

3. PERIMETER SHAPE (or *Silhouette*)
- Wide front allows a skier to turn hard while standing on the nose of the ski without falling forward; it's also easier to deep-water start
- Wide tails work well for a skier who rides the ski far back; more surface area improves the acceleration for a tail rider
- Wide midsections turn easier due to the large flat pivot point (center), but this type of midsection makes it harder for the ski to hold an edge
- Narrow fronts drop into the water more easily during the turn, but will throw a skier forward off the ski if his weight is too far forward
- Narrow tails are usually slower as they sit deeper in the water

- Narrow midsections roll from edge to edge easier and are more suitable to holding a hard edge

4. ROCKER SHAPE

- Continuous rocker turns easier with a skier's weight on the tail
- A flat section in the overall rocker makes the ski more stable and works well for a skier who rides forward
- Tail rocker slows a ski down but enables a skier to turn more easily
- Less tail rocker allows the ski to accelerate faster but is harder to turn

5. FLEX

- Soft skis turn a little more easily compared to stiff skis
- Stiff skis have more acceleration but are harder to turn
- Soft flex will allow a skier to move around on the ski more without falling; stiff flex gets the skier through the wakes faster and allows the skier more time to set up for the turn

FLEX

6. FIN SHAPES

- Flat front edge holds the tip of the ski up
- Round front edge pushes the tip down
- Cutoff back edge allows ski to pivot more quickly

FIN SHAPES

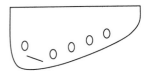

Flat leading edge

As for the fins on the bottom of the skis, intermediate and competition-type slalom skis have a deeper fin than those found on combo skis. A lot of high-end slalom skis come with wings on the fin. (Remember the winged keel on the America's Cup boats? Same idea.) A wing can help a recreational skier, especially in the stability of a turn, but you really have to work with it for a few sets to feel comfortable.

To learn to ski with a wing, start with it parallel to the bottom of the ski. As you get accustomed to using the added drag of the wing to slow down, you can turn it down a few degrees. My advice, though, is to forget about the wings for now and concentrate on having fun. Some pro skiers don't even use wings on some of their skis.

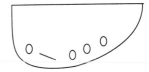

Round leading edge

The angle of the wing on advanced skis can be adjusted; the more angle, the more the ski will slow down.

BINDINGS

There are several different types of bindings, and when you're ready to purchase a slalom ski you should know the differences. The least expensive bindings are made out of thin rubber and don't have any foam or softening pads to cushion the foot, nor do they offer much support. Some won't even have holes for your fingers so that you can grasp them to help get your foot inside. These bindings are usually adjustable: either the toe piece stays fixed while the heel piece slides forward, or vice versa. Sometimes they are mounted directly on the ski rather than on a plate. You will see these types on lower end, beginning skis and even on some intermediate skis.

A step up is a binding that is still adjustable but is affixed to an aluminum or plastic plate. The plate will be narrow and a little longer than the binding. This type of adjustable binding will be a little sturdier and will have an adjustment mechanism such as a flip lock or screw-in device. The binding may come with or without ankle wraps, which offer the ankle a little more support by using a long rubber piece that crisscrosses around the ankle and is adjusted with a Velcro-type closure.

High-performance bindings come in sizes ranging from extra small to extra large. Some companies, such as O'Brien, also have bindings for women's narrower and smaller feet. High-performance bindings that the pros use have double-high wraps—

Bindings come in a variety of materials and designs, from the basic, adjustable bindings of beginner skis to the double-high wrap of advanced skis. Bottom to top: intermediate Velcro wrap, advanced double-high wrap, beginner adjustable with no wrap.

strips of heavy rubber that go around the ankle in both directions. These bindings are usually difficult to get on in the water, since they fit so snugly. The key is to be sure your foot and the binding are both really wet before you put them on. You might also need to add a little biodegradable dish-washing soap or a special lubricating agent (made by most ski companies) inside to make sure your foot will slide right in. Pro skiers like their bindings very tight (our feet often go numb after wearing them for long periods of time) because they give us the most support and control of the ski and still pop off if we take a hard fall.

Deciding whether to have an open-toe rear binding, or a double-high wrap binding for your back foot depends on which deepwater start method you use. If you start, as I do, with your back foot dragging in the water, you will have to have an open-toe rear binding.

YOUR SKIING STYLE

When you're buying an advanced or intermediate ski it's helpful to know the skiing style you have developed. There are three basic styles common to slalom skiing.

A C-turning style describes a skier who shifts his weight to the front of the ski for smooth, carving turns. The ski turns smoothly and symmetrically on both sides. The skier will follow the arc of the ski tip through the turn, rather than trying to force the ski to get more angle. It's a very smooth and rhythmic way of turning. This type of skier would want to ride a ski that is a bit wide in front, with a medium nose rocker, a flat midsection, and a moderately wide tunnel on the bottom.

The tight-carving (or TC) style skier is one who skis in a neutral position with the weight balanced over the middle of the ski. When this type of skier turns, he tends to shift his weight to the tail of the ski to accelerate. This is also a symmetrical and smooth style of turning even though it tends to look a little more aggressive than C style.

The ski for this type of skier will have a little narrower front; moderate flex throughout the ski; continuous rocker; small, round bevels; a moderately wide midsection; and a coke bottle–shaped tail. This skier may find a combination of different bevels works better because he skis in the middle and on the back of the ski.

Then there's the Z-type skier. This is the skier who skis from point to point with quick, pivoting turns and rides the back of the ski because the ski is always accelerating. This is one of the most radical skiing styles because the skier usually has a lot of power out of the turns without the smooth symmetry the C or TC skiers have. As an example, I'm a Z-style skier on my "turn-to-the-left" or bad side and a TC skier on my "turn-to-the-right" good side.

The ski for Z-style skiers will be narrow in the front and midsection, stiff in the tail, and the bevels will be sharp and severe. The combination of stiff flex and large, sharp bevels with a flat leading edge gives the ski added lift out of the water for

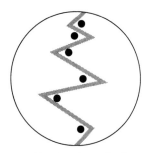

Turning the path of
Z-turn type skier

Turning path of
C-turn type skier

Turning the path of
TC-turn type skier

speed when crossing the wakes from buoy to buoy. These skiers generally benefit from a wing because it helps them slow down.

You'll find a few new skis on the market that manufacturers claim are designed for women. More often than not, it's nothing more than a change of graphics that allows the manufacturer to market a ski to women. A ski that is truly designed for a woman should be a little lighter in weight, a bit narrower, and not quite as stiff as some of the men's skis. The bindings should be downsized for women, and the ski bevels should be a little smaller and sharper. In general, women are TC-type skiers, so this is the type of ski they need.

The Camille Pro line of skis that I designed with O'Brien takes all these things into consideration. We made the skis light in weight and not quite as stiff because women generally aren't quite as strong or as heavy as men. The bindings are downsized to fit women's feet. The semi-sharp bevels guide the ski smoothly through the turns and won't allow the ski to go deep into the water during the turn. The combination of all these factors makes a ski that women don't have to force to work.

BUYER BEWARE

When you go into a ski shop to buy your skis, don't hesitate to ask for help. Obviously, the salespeople will want to sell you the brand the shop carries, and there may be nothing wrong with this. However, you should buy a ski that works with your style, and one way to do this is to take a video of yourself skiing and show it to a knowledgeable salesperson. This will help the sales staff determine what will be best for you. Don't be afraid to ask questions. Don't buy a ski for the bells and whistles, the graphics, colors, and gimmicks. You should be more concerned with the type of bottom design, how the bevels work, and whether or not the bindings fit you properly.

A lot of ski shops have demo programs, and you should take advantage of them. They allow you to put down a deposit, pick up a couple of different skis, and try them out before you buy. Take into consideration the ski you've been using and what type of water you generally ski on, rough or calm.

Larger skis will have more surface area, so they're easier to get up on and to ski on rough water, but you will sacrifice performance. A shorter or smaller ski will allow you to turn a little tighter and more quickly. Balance your needs with the ski's function and you should get a perfect match.

Manufacturers designate skis as intermediate and advanced for a reason. If you've just learned to slalom you could do more harm than good and interfere with the fun of skiing by jumping right on to an advanced ski. Buy an intermediate ski first and master it before moving up.

EXTRAS—GLOVES, WETSUITS, AND MORE

After a season or two on the water, you will start thinking of ways to stretch and enhance your skiing season. If you are, there are a few accessories available that will enhance your skiing fun and performance.

GLOVES

A good pair of ski gloves may make a world of difference in your skiing endurance and performance. They are excellent protection from blisters, especially if you don't ski regularly enough to build calluses. The gloves, made of chamois-like material, should be fairly snug when you try them on in the store because they will stretch in the water. They may even feel a bit small the first time you ski, but they'll stretch. I actually use two pairs of gloves when I ski—a thin pair and a thick, well-padded pair over them. This is comparable to wearing two pairs of socks when you run to help prevent blisters. As with vests, most ski companies make gloves to match their skis. Because they make your grip feel more secure, gloves can sometimes be the psychological edge skiers need when they're learning deep-water slalom starts.

WETSUITS

If your skiing season is cut short by cool weather, you can extend it by using a wetsuit. Wetsuits are neoprene rubber suits that help retain body heat. The skintight suit allows a thin coating

of water next to your body, which is then warmed by your body heat. The neoprene acts as an insulator, keeping the warm water and heat in even though you're wet—thus, the term *wetsuit*. Wetsuits have evolved from the original, bulky black skins they once were to sophisticated styles and cuts designed for specific sports.

The most common style used for skiing is a "shorty" design, with sleeves to just above the elbow and legs to just above the knees. They are usually made in a combination of thicknesses, so the body of the suit itself is two millimeters while the sleeves are only one millimeter and thus more flexible. Another popular style with cold-water skiers is the long john, with full-length sleeves and legs. There are also wetsuits designed like swimsuits for women, and wetsuit shorts that look like biking pants. These are great protection during those unexpected falls. If you can't decide what style to choose, talk to more experienced skiers in your area and find out what they use.

Wetsuits come in a variety of thicknesses, typically ranging from 1 to 5 millimeters. The thicker the suit, the warmer it will be, and the more restrictive. Personally, I feel if you need a

Wetsuits and drysuits offer warmth and comfort on cold days as well as protection from hypothermia. They are available in styles suited for all weather conditions, from the "shortie" I'm wearing to the ultra-warm drysuit on the left, which has watertight gaskets at the extremities.

ESSENTIAL EQUIPMENT

5-millimeter suit, it's probably not worth it—wait for warmer days. But I live in Florida, and I'm a wimp when it comes to cold weather!

It's very important to buy a sport-specific suit. Wetsuits today have various combinations of neoprene and other materials to accommodate the predominant stress areas of specific sports. A windsurfer, a surfer, and a water skier will each need a different type of suit, as each of these sports requires flexibility in different areas. Add to this the suits designed for specific disciplines within a sport (such as a barefoot suit or a jump suit in water skiing), and you can see how choices can be critical—and confusing.

The suit you choose for water skiing should be snug but flexible; it may even feel tight when you try it on in the store. Short sleeves that extend to mid-biceps are preferred; long sleeves tend to restrict the blood flow and can cause your arms to tire quickly, but if it's cold you may need them.

Additional flex points for water skiing are the knees and buttocks. Some companies add high-performance material, such as Bion (a stretchy breathable material developed for medical uses) in the joints, for more freedom of movement. Check for freedom of movement in the shoulders and knees when you try on your suit. Some companies also add ankle or thigh cinches to prevent water from rushing up the legs.

Water-ski suits come with zipper closures, front or back. I prefer a back zipper, which has a long ribbon attached, because the front-zipper style can be a challenge to get in and out of when wet.

Some suits, particularly barefoot suits and jump suits, come with built-in flotation, just like that used in PFDs. (These new jump suits are a great improvement over the cutoff jeans we used to wear back in the sixties!) Most wetsuit companies are awaiting Coast Guard approval for their "flotation" suits, even though a few have obtained it as of this writing. So you must remember to wear a life jacket over a suit that doesn't have Coast Guard–approved built-in flotation.

Wetsuits will vary widely in cost, depending on the type you purchase and where you purchase it. You should expect to spend no less than $150 for a quality suit, and up to $395 or more for "specialty" suits.

A good intermediate choice for cold weather is the long-leg, long-sleeve suit. If you insist on skiing in heavy-duty cold weather, you'll have to look into the purchase of a drysuit. Unlike the wetsuit, the drysuit is made with rubber gaskets at all the openings for the extremities, and is literally designed to keep you dry. Often you can wear silk underwear or leggings under these suits to add warmth. The only type of drysuit I'd recommend for skiing is made of heavy-duty neoprene, which looks like a one-size-too-large wetsuit, with gasket closures at the neck, hands, and feet and a waterproof zipper across the shoulders. I don't recommend the "baggie" kind of drysuit because if it's punctured it can quickly fill with water.

SAFETY GEAR AND TOYS

Another handy accessory that adds safety to your skiing is a ski rope "shock absorber." This is a piece of foam that fits over the ski rope so that if the skier unexpectedly pops or loses the handle hard enough for it to fling back into the boat, it won't hit the driver or observer. Larger skiers using stretchy ropes have been known to exert such force on the rope that a flying handle pops back through the windshield of the boat.

If you have children, you're definitely going to want to get caught up in the kneeboard craze. These simple boards, which look a lot like short, fat surfboards, are really easy and fun for kids to ride. So are tubes that can be pulled behind the boat. And would-be surfers can try their luck with ski-boards—surfboard type of board designed to be pulled behind the boat.

Out of all the toys available, kneeboards are probably the most popular among children because they are easy and less intimidating than skis. A child simply kneels on the board, which has a sort of safety belt on it, and holds on to the rope to be pulled. There are dozens of models available. Start with a beginner's board and be sure there's adequate padding for comfort. Most kneeboards are fairly indestructible and should last a long time.

QUICK TIPS

- Perimeter shape, bottom design, bevels, rocker, flex, and fin shape work together to make a ski perform a certain way.

- Various ski shapes are designed for different skiing styles.
- Skiing styles may be C or carving turns, TC or tight-carving turns, Z with quick pivoting turns, or a combination thereof.
- C-type skis are wider in front with smooth, rounded bevels. C skiers tend to ride the front of the ski.
- TC-type skis are narrower in front with a moderately wide midsection. TC skiers ride over the middle of the ski.
- Z-type skis have a narrow front and midsection with a deep tunnel. Z skiers ride the back of the ski, and winged fins can help them slow down at turns.
- There are a variety of styles of wetsuits available for all weather conditions.

SKIING BASICS

WARMING UP

Now that you've got your boat and equipment lined up, you're ready to hit the water and have some fun.

First, take some time to warm up a little. Warming up is important in all sports, but especially in skiing because you can't ease into it. Once the boat starts to pull, you're on your way, and falls can occur very quickly. If you miscalculate and hit a wake the wrong way, there's no time to correct the mistake; you go down instantly.

I try to make sure every part of my body is loose before I ski. Everyone should do some type of stretching routine for all the major muscle groups. The following is my regular stretching routine, step by step. It is based on my many years of skiing and knowledge about the types of injuries that can happen. You may choose to modify this routine by adding extra stretches for your tighter muscles, but you should include at least the basics.

Neck: rolling and rotating

Shoulders: hunch up and down, bring forward and back, cross hands to stretch out and warm up area between shoulder blades (Note: stretching shoulders is especially important because they take most of the pull and strain of skiing.)

Hands and fingers: pull fingertips back and stretch (A good grip is your life line when skiing.)

Chest: balance pulling effects of skiing with some pushing exercises, such as leaning against the dock and doing mock push-ups, or loop your ski handle and rope around a tree or dock support, get in skiing position and pull as if skiing

Knee to chest curls: pull knee toward chest to stretch and warm up lower back, drop knees from side to side, and do a few ab crunches (The lower back takes plenty of stress and strong abdominals will help with support.)

Lower back stretch: in modified yoga position, roll over backwards

Hamstrings and inner thighs: runner's stretch

Calf raises: stand on edge of dock and drop heels below dock level and lift up on toes

An additional stretching routine to warm up is passive stretching with a buddy.

PROPER BODY POSITION— START ON DRY LAND

I was only four years old when I first learned to ski. My father, an avid water skier, was eager for me to participate in family ski weekends. He also knew that the basic foundation for building good, solid, water-skiing skills is proper body position. That first weekend he showed me the procedures—from putting on skis to getting up—on dry land first.

No matter what your age, and no matter how impatient you are to go for that first run, the very best place to learn to ski initially is on dry land. It's the easiest way to perfect your body position and to feel comfortable and assured about what you are doing.

Assuming you've never skied before (if you're already a slalom skier, you can move on to Chapter 3), it is easier to learn on two skis than one. If you are with someone who has skied before, his or her experience may make things easier, but it's not necessary.

First things first. Set the skis side by side on the shore. Wet

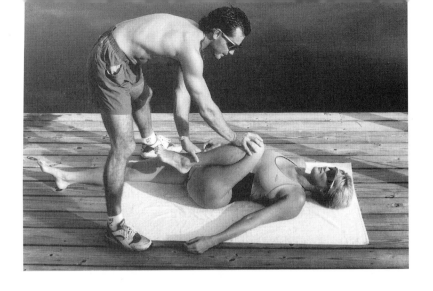

A: *Passive stretching with a buddy is a good way to ensure you'll remember to stretch every time. This bent-knee-to-chest stretch works the lower back.*

B: *Extended leg stretches help the hamstrings. Remember to let your partner know your point of pain.*

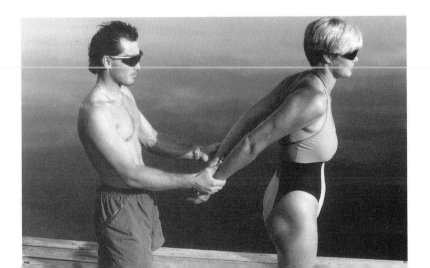

C: *Don't forget to stretch your arms. Passive stretching with a buddy may help you stretch farther than you can on your own.*

A   B

the bindings and slip your feet in by pulling aside the heel rubber and working your foot as far into the front toe piece as is comfortable and then pull the heel on. Then adjust the bindings so they fit snugly. Once your feet are snug inside your bindings, simply sit down on the backs of the skis. Take the rope handle in your hands with a double overhand grip—palms facing downward. Ask someone to stand in front of you and hold the rope taut for you. Extend your arms so that they are straight and on either side of your knees. This is the position you'll take in the water.

The person holding the rope plays a key role: he or she must keep tension on the rope at all times just as the boat will on the water. To simulate an actual deep-water start, keep your arms and back straight and allow the rope to pull you up—use your legs as if you were getting up out of a chair without using your arms for leverage. The person holding the rope should pull it gradually until you are standing up straight, with your knees slightly bent.

Once you are standing, mentally check your body position. Proper body position means feeling balanced, and it's easier to teach your body that balance point on shore than on the water. Your feet should be about shoulder-width apart. Your weight should be balanced on the balls of your feet, not on your heels and not on your toes. Your ankles should be bent forward, which

C

A: *For dryland practice, have someone hold the rope for you and start in a sitting position, arms straight, knees to chest.*

B: *Use your legs to stand up as the person helping you pulls on the rope.*

C: *Check your body position once you're up: knees bent, arms straight, back straight, and shoulders back.*

will in turn push your knees forward. Soft flexible knees, always bent, are very important in all phases of water skiing because they act as shock absorbers, smoothing out bumps and helping you keep your balance on the water.

Your hips should be aligned over your knees, or as close as possible, not sticking out behind you. Your back should be straight and strong, held firm with your abdominal muscles. There should be no arch or bend in the back, and your arms should be straight with shoulders rolled back, not pulled in toward you, to start. Your posture from the waist up should be "regal."

Your head should be level, with your eyes on the horizon. As tempting as it will be to look down at your feet, you must remember the axiom: if you look down, you fall down.

Go through this process of being pulled up and then mentally checking out your body position several times on dry land. When you feel confident that your body position is right, it's time to get in the water.

UNIVERSAL SIGNALS

Before you ski the first time, you and your driver should both know the universal hand signals that have been developed so that skiers can communicate with the people in the boat. (By the way, most states require an aft-facing observer when a boat is pulling a skier. The observer's job is to communicate to the boat driver what's going on with the skier.)

The skier's hand signals are as follows:

- Thumbs up means go a little faster; thumbs down means slow down.
- A slicing motion across the neck means cut the engine.
- Patting the top of the head means "head in," back to your point of origin.
- When you fall, a wave of one hand over your head signals the driver that you're okay.

The driver can also communicate with you by hand signals:

- When the driver raises his index finger in the air and waves his hand in a circle, he's turning the boat around.
- When he moves his hand in a wavy motion, there's rough water ahead, probably wakes from another boat.

If you ski often with the same driver, you'll become accustomed to each other's signals and may be able to read lips (exaggerated of course!) or add a shoulder shrug to ask a question.

GETTING INTO THE WATER

Always start your skiing where the water is reasonably deep. If you ski where you can touch bottom, it can be dangerous if you take a bad spill. You never know what might be on the bottom, and there's no point in risking injury.

When you first get in the water, ask your driver to take up the slack in the rope by idling away until the ski rope is taut. It must be taut before you begin, because the handle will pop out of your hands like a slingshot if the driver takes off when there's too much slack in the rope.

READY, SET, GO

Once the rope is taut, concentrate on your body position in the water. Your arms are around your knees. About 12 inches of your ski tips should be out of the water at about a 45-degree angle to the surface of the water. You probably won't feel completely balanced the first few times you do this, but when you do feel reasonably balanced signal the driver to pull you up by yelling "okay" or "hit it." It's not a good idea to use the word *go* because it can be understood as "no."

If you have trouble getting balanced or you float over onto your belly with the skis behind you while the driver is idling to tighten the rope, just stand straight up on your skis, keeping them underwater, as if you were on land until the rope is taut and then get back into position. It can be very helpful to use the standing-on-skis position if you are dealing with an inexperienced boat driver or if for some reason it takes the boat a few moments to get into position.

Let me mention here that it can be especially difficult for small children to balance their skis. To help, you can make a game out of it by just playing "balance" at the water's edge or even in a swimming pool, so they tread water while holding the skis in proper starting position. This will also relieve some of the child's anxiety the first time he goes out to ski.

Your driver should make certain you're lined up directly behind the boat because if you're off to one side the pull won't be gradual; you'll be snatched out of the water and on to one side or over the front of your skis.

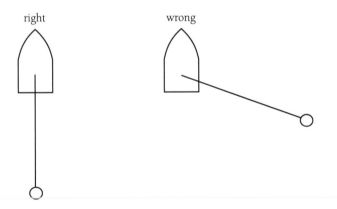

The driver should make certain the skier is centered behind the boat before starting.

As soon as you tell the driver to hit it, he will make every effort to accelerate smoothly and steadily. You should concentrate on maintaining correct body position until the skis actually break the surface of the water and begin to plane. Waiting a beat, use your legs to stand up, just as you practiced on dry land. Keep

A

B

A: When you are in the correct position in the water—knees to chest, arms straight, rope between the skis, and the rope is taut—you are ready to ski.

B: Keep your knees well bent and your weight centered over the skis as you come up, using your legs . . .

your eyes on the horizon or the boat, and your arms out straight with shoulders rolled back and your back straight. The transition from sitting on the skis to standing should be one smooth motion. Don't straighten your knees; concentrate on keeping your ankles bent and knees flexed. And resist the temptation to look down.

COMMON ERRORS

Everyone learning to ski for the first time will make at least one of these mistakes. Don't worry—they are all easily corrected.

If you stand up too quickly and straighten your knees, you will be pulled forward off the skis onto your face and into what skiers call a face plant. To correct this, concentrate on staying in your crouched position a little longer, and stand up gradually. When my students stand up too quickly I always tell them to count to five slowly as the boat begins to pull them and then stand up.

Another common mistake is pulling the rope in toward the chest as you feel the pull of the boat. This will cause the skis to shoot out from under you toward the boat and you'll fall over the back of your skis. To correct this problem, concentrate on

CAMILLE DUVALL

C

D

keeping your arms straight and your back straight and firm. Think of a proud or regal posture. Keep your shoulders pulled back, rather than rolled forward, and let your legs do the work.

Sometimes a skier will pull the rope toward himself as the boat starts and then suddenly straighten his arms as the full pull of the boat is felt. This generally results in a forward fall as the skier is pulled forward out of the skis like a slingshot. To avoid this mistake, concentrate on keeping your arms straight when the boat starts to pull, and if you do find yourself with bent arms, straighten them out *slowly!*

If the skis are tucked up underneath you too far, rather than positioned in front of you, the skis will be left behind when the boat starts to pull. This also happens if your back is bent forward rather than straight and firm. Focus on holding your back erect and getting the skis out in front of you while keeping the knees bent as you're getting up.

If the problem is falling to either side, you are putting too much weight on one foot rather than weighting each foot equally.

Once you're up and skiing, mentally check your body position just as you practiced on shore. Correct any mistakes slowly. Skiing will feel effortless if you're in the proper body position. If you're not, you'll feel strained and awkward.

On your premier ski run, it's best to ski directly behind the

C: Gradually begin to stand up . . .

D: . . . until you are in the proper body position for skiing. Notice that my shoulders are pulled back and my back is straight.

boat, between the two wakes, getting used to how the skis feel and how your knees act as shock absorbers on bumpy water. If you're feeling comfortable and confident, you may want to start trying to zig and zag a little. To do this, put a little more weight on the ski opposite to the direction you want to go and be careful to maintain your body position at all times. Point your skis in the direction you want to go, put pressure on the outer ski, and you'll be surprised how easy it is to maneuver.

To stop edging or zigzagging, simply relieve the pressure and you'll stop going in that direction.

CROSSING THE WAKES

Once you've mastered edging your skis, start going outside the wakes in both directions. As you cross the wakes, it will feel like going over a speed bump in a car. While skiing over the wakes, mentally reinforce correct body position. Avoid letting the bump of the wake cause you to bend your back. You can correct this problem by exaggerating the bend of your knees and allowing them to act as shock absorbers to the wake. Bent knees will help you maintain your balance when any number of problems arise. If you snow ski (or do any other sport) you know it's impossible to maintain your balance with stiff legs.

Once you're outside the wake, the water will be much smoother. You'll feel the pull of the boat trying to tug you back to the middle of the wake, so go with it. Point your skis in the direction you want to go, add weight to the outside ski, and cross over the wake.

It's much easier to cross the wakes if your skis are on an angle to the wake, and if you keep them together. Don't try to step over the wake one ski at a time, with the skis pointing toward the boat. While this may seem less frightening than just zooming over the wake all at once, the reality is that you are much more likely to fall if you try it, as the skis will split on either side of the wake, and you'll spread-eagle into the water.

Each skill you learn is a building block. Ski on combo skis until you are so comfortable crossing back and forth across both wakes that proper body position is automatic. When you reach this stage, you're ready to kick off a ski and learn to slalom.

To cross the wakes successfully, you must learn to steer by using pressure on the ski opposite the direction you want to go. Concentrate on keeping your knees bent but flexible; point your skis toward the wake and ski over the wake with both skis at the same time.

DROPPING A SKI—BACK TO DRY LAND

Before you learn to drop a ski, you need to figure out which foot will be your "front foot" and remain forward on the single ski. It doesn't matter which one; you should use whichever leg feels most comfortable. It might be the leg you use to kick a ball, or the one you instinctively put forward to maintain your balance when gently shoved from behind. If neither of these tests instinctively yields a front foot, you can get a feel for which leg is more comfortable in the forward position while skiing on two skis. Try shifting your weight to one ski; gently lift the tip of the other ski

To get a feel for what it will be like on one ski, try lifting a ski with tip up slightly when you ski with two. You may switch back and forth, lifting first one ski, then the other, until you are sure which leg is most comfortable and the more stable of the two.

up and slightly off the water. Repeat this on the other side and you'll discover which one feels most stable. This is the one you'll put in the front binding on the single ski.

Once you've determined which foot will be forward, go back on shore and put both skis on, making sure that the ski with the back binding is on your dominant foot. Adjust the binding of the foot that will be your back foot so it's reasonably loose. Stand in the proper body position you've practiced. Having someone hold the rope taut will help you keep your balance.

Check your body position: your arms should be straight out, your back straight and firm, knees and ankles bent and flexible enough to absorb the shock of the wakes. Hold the handle with a baseball bat-type grip—one hand up, one under, hands slightly apart. Some coaches and professional skiers suggest a good way to determine which hand is "up" on this grip is to make it the one opposite the forward foot.

Now practice dropping your ski. First, maintaining proper body position, shift your weight to the leg of the forward foot. Gently raise the heel of the foot that will be dropping a ski—keep your head erect, your shoulders level, and your eyes on the horizon. Point your toe and slide your foot out of the binding in one smooth motion. Still keeping your eyes up, mentally check your body position again. It should be exactly the same as what you learned on combo skis, except all your weight will be on the one leg. To compensate for the initial instability, you'll need to exaggerate the bend in the knee of the leg on the ski.

The real key to learning to ski on one ski is the shifting of your weight. Always shift your weight first, then drop the ski. When the bindings are wet, the ski will slip off more easily than on dry land. And don't worry about getting hit by the ski because you will leave it behind as soon as you're out of it.

The biggest mistake first-time slalom skiers seem to make is trying to cram the back foot into the back binding too quickly. Resist this temptation, and continue to concentrate on keeping your balance on the forward leg. Let your free leg help you balance.

Before attempting this on water, you should practice putting your foot in the back toe binding while on land so your body will know how to respond. Focus your balance on the front leg and smoothly and gradually place your free foot against the calf of the front leg. Gradually slide that foot down the calf until it touches the back binding. Keeping your weight on the front leg, gently slide your toes into the back binding. Once your foot is in the binding, you can smoothly shift your weight until you are balanced on both legs. The key to success is knowing where your weight is balanced and making gradual, smooth movements as opposed to sudden, jerky ones.

After you've practiced on land a few times, take your knowledge to the water. Be sure that the ski with the back toe binding is on the foot that will be forward. Adjust the binding on the ski to be dropped to a very large size so it slips off easily but not so loose it falls off as you start. Get up on two skis and be comfortable before you drop the ski. When you're balanced and you've checked your body position, you're ready to go. First, shift your

A

B

A: To drop a ski, first shift your weight to the ski you will be skiing on.

B: Point the toe of the foot that will drop the ski and it will slip out of the loosened binding.

weight to the front leg. When you're comfortably balanced—with the knee bent—point the toe of your other foot and allow the ski to glide off. Don't shake the ski off—you'll lose your balance. It's important to remember *not to look at the ski you're dropping. When you look down, you fall down.* Keep your eyes forward; you'll feel when the ski is off.

Once the ski is off, concentrate on your balance. Bend your front knee and let your other foot hang loose until you are comfortable; don't drag the loose foot in the water. Don't panic and try to ram the loose foot into the back binding. Remember what you practiced on land and rest the back foot against the calf, ankle, or heel of the front leg until you feel ready to slide it gently into the back binding. Once it's in, shift your weight slowly until you are balanced on both feet.

Practice keeping your balance as you ski directly behind the boat. Once you've mastered this, try to weave gently from side to side without leaning your upper body. As you weave, you should be nearing the boat wakes but not crossing over them. Check your body position frequently: arms straight, shoulders rolled back, back strong, abdominal muscles firm, knees and ankles well bent, and back heel flat against the ski.

If you can't keep your back heel against the ski, your bindings

C

D

may be too far apart. Most pro skiers ski with the toes of the back foot touching the back of the front binding. Although you can bring your skis to a shop, it's easy (and less expensive) to make the adjustment yourself. Check your ski on the dock before you go out, and if necessary adjust the binding by removing the screws around the back toe binding's plate and shifting the plate forward using the holes provided for this purpose. Then put the screws back into the original holes.

If you don't have a plate for your rear binding, you must remove the screws, move the binding forward (after measuring the correct distance with your foot), and drill directly through the screw holes in the binding frame. (Use extra caution when drilling since it's easy to drill through a ski.) Then, use two-part epoxy to fill the unused holes. You'll need to move your nonskid (the sandpaper-like substance which keeps your rear foot from sliding around) forward as well. Finally, simply replace the screws. You will know that your bindings are properly spaced, if someone pushes you gently while your feet are in the bindings and you are able to maintain your balance.

If you fall while attempting to drop a ski, have the driver retrieve your dropped ski and try again. Once you feel comfortable on a slalom ski, you are ready to try getting up on one ski.

C: The ski will slide away. Keep your weight centered on the ski as you gradually position the other leg. Slide your foot down your calf to find the back binding.

D: Gradually shift your weight to both feet only after your foot is secure in the back binding. If you put too much weight on your back heel, the ski will be riding on its tail and feel unstable.

SKIING BASICS

47

STARTING OUT
IN DEEP WATER

There are two methods for deep-water starts on one ski, and advocates of each will argue endlessly that their method is best. I advise trying both, then continuing with the one that seems most comfortable for you. The difference between these two methods is the placement of your back foot. Some skiers prefer to start with the back foot out of its binding and dragging behind them to help with balance, like a boat rudder, until they're up and going. Others start with both feet in the bindings, which I feel requires a little more strength and puts a bit more strain on your back.

Either way, the starting position is the same: knees bent and close to the chest; arms straight out, not pulled in to the chest; shoulders rolled back; back straight; and abdominal muscles strong. It is crucial to keep your back straight and resist the power of the boat; otherwise you'll be pulled out over the front of the ski. Keep in mind that you have only half the surface area to get up on as you had with two skis.

If your boat is slow to plane off, you have to hold your perfect body position longer before you're pulled up out of the water, because the boat will drag you some distance in the water before planing off. Skiers with more powerful boats usually succeed at deep-water starts more quickly because the boat gets them on top of the water faster.

The boat driver plays a crucial role in the success or failure of the deep-water start. A driver should never attempt to pull a skier up until the ski towrope is stretched out taut in a straight line directly behind the boat. The rope should be lined up straight off the pylon or towing eye where it's attached, whether it's in the center of the boat or on the transom. Most important, the driver needs to watch how quickly a skier comes up and adjust the throttle pressure to suit the reactions of the skier. Drivers of real ski boats and other powerful boats should exercise caution so as to not rip the skier out of the water. The pull up should be gentle.

Towing speed is determined by the weight and size of the skier. As a rule of thumb, speed for a beginner shouldn't exceed 20 mph for skiers weighing up to 100 pounds; 25 mph for 100 to 160 pounds; 30 mph for more than 160 pounds. However,

For a deep-water start with both feet in the bindings, put the ski at a 45-degree angle, bend your knees to your chest, and keep your shoulders rolled back.

the skier can signal the driver to speed up (thumbs up), or slow down (thumbs down).

The most common mistake made by skiers attempting their first deep-water start is not keeping a straight back. Often, the skier doesn't anticipate the added drag of being on one ski, or the power of the boat. To avoid bending at the waist when the boat accelerates, concentrate on keeping the shoulders rolled back, the arms extended straight, and the abdominals tight.

If you're skiing with your right foot forward, start with the rope to the left of your ski. If you're skiing with your left foot forward, the rope should be on the right side of the ski. This helps keep the ski pointed at the boat while the rope is getting tight as well as for the initial pull up out of the water. As the boat takes off, your leg (or legs, if both feet are in the bindings) should stay bent, resisting the pressure that the water puts against the ski. Once you feel the ski start to plane off, you can increase the

A

B

pressure of your leg or legs on the ski until you are in skiing position.

Some skiers hold the handle with a baseball-bat grip (one palm up, the other down), while others prefer both palms down. Do whichever is comfortable for you to start, but remember that once you start cutting back and forth through the wake, you'll have to switch to the baseball-bat grip.

COMMON PROBLEMS

Sometimes the drag of the ski seems an impossible barrier to overcome, and skiers tire quickly and become discouraged. If this happens to you, check the angle of your ski in the water. It should not stick straight up, 90 degrees to the surface of the water. This totally defeats the desired planing effect of the ski. The ski should be angled about 45 degrees to the surface of the water. If it's too horizontal or flat, you will be thrown off balance, or the pull of the boat will be so strong the handle will be yanked out of your hands. Another solution is to keep your back foot out of the binding, dragging it for balance as you are pulled up. With this method, the ski might feel a little easier to manage.

C

D

Sometimes the reverse is true, and you may feel more comfortable with both feet in. Just go with what feels best.

If you find yourself falling over backward when attempting a deep-water start, or if the ski starts wobbling from side to side, chances are your front leg is too straight. Remember to keep those knees bent, up close to your chest.

C: Here the back foot is dragging behind for balance.

D: Once the back foot is in the binding, check proper body position.

BEACH STARTS

A beach start may be easier for you to learn than the traditional deep-water start, but it's not something that is generally done on two skis. One reason many skiers want to learn a beach start is that it is a particularly good start method when the water's cold and you don't want to get wet.

The term *beach start* is really a misnomer—it would be more apt to call it a shallow-water start. The key to the beach start is timing, and good driving is essential. To do a beach start, walk out to water about mid-thigh in depth. (Note: You won't want to try this in a busy waterway or where there are lots of obstructions —docks, logs, rocks, or vicious dogs—nearby.) Coil one or two loops of the ski rope in your hand as if you were beginning to

In a deep-water start with one foot out of the binding, remember to bend both knees and keep your back straight, shoulders rolled back.

put it away. Have the driver idle away to make the rest of the rope taut; he can do this a little faster than he would if you were in deep water. Yell "okay" to the driver a split second before the rope is tight, (you may have to hold the rope near your waist to take up slack for timing's sake), and push off the bottom with the free foot, shifting your weight from the bottom onto the foot with the ski on it. Keep your back straight and strong and the pull of the boat won't feel too abrupt as the driver accelerates quickly to skiing speed. This start can be difficult at first because the boat literally yanks you off the beach. Remember that learning a beach start takes practice, a good driver, and timing.

Another popular start method is the dock start. It is basically

A: A beach start, or shallow-water start, begins with some slack in the rope.

B: Let the boat idle out to take up the slack. You may have to hold the last bit of slack low on your hips.

C: As the rope becomes taut, tell the driver to "hit it" and shift your weight from the bottom onto your ski.

D: Resist the pull of the boat by keeping your shoulders rolled back and your back very straight.

E: Be sure to keep your weight shifted away from the boat when the speed is still fairly slow. This position will help you resist the pull of the boat and help make up for any timing errors on the part of the driver.

done in the same fashion as a beach start, but from a dock. It may be done in a standing or sitting position. The timing and boat driving are all done exactly the same way as on a beach start. Don't even attempt the dock start unless the dock has no obstructions near it.

I once had a group of students attend my ski school who wanted to spend the whole week learning different slalom start methods. We spent an entire morning trying to learn beach starts, and then they decided dock starts would be easier. Unfortunately, the concept of "timing" was foreign to these students, and the whole affair looked like a replay of NFL bloopers. They fell every way you can imagine. They just couldn't get the timing down.

I suggested we break for lunch and try again in the afternoon. The students relaxed during lunch and seemed eager to try again. When we reassembled on the dock, they got a little extra motivation from an unexpected source. A few days earlier, someone on the lake had apparently shot and killed (illegally) a very large (12-foot) gator, but hadn't managed to get it out of the water. Just as the first student was about to try another dock start, the carcass floated to the surface right in front of the dock! Not only did that student succeed on his first attempt, so did all the rest. That's what I call performance under pressure.

QUICK TIPS

- Warm up before skiing to avoid injury.
- Never stretch past the point of pain.
- Practice body position on land first—knees bent, back straight, arms straight, shoulders rolled back, abdominal muscles firm.
- Binding adjustment should be snug but not so tight that circulation is cut off.
- Make sure driver, skier, and observer know and use universal hand signals: thumbs up for "faster," thumbs down for "slower," slicing motion across neck for "cut the engine," patting top of head for "head in." Say "hit it" or "okay" when ready to ski since "go" can sound like "no." Observer should say "fall" when a skier goes down.
- Boat speed for beginning skiers shouldn't exceed 20 mph for skiers weighing up to 100 pounds; 25 mph for 100 to 160 pounds; 30 mph for more than 160 pounds when learning.
- Before the start: rope should be taut, skier should be in the proper body position with skis in front, about 12 inches out of the water and at a 45-degree angle, arms on either side of bent knees and out straight, back straight, shoulders rolled back.

- Common errors to avoid in the start: standing up too quickly and straightening knees, pulling rope into chest, or pulling rope in, then letting it out suddenly.
- Crossing wakes: bend knees; use them as shock absorbers.
- To drop a ski: before starting, loosen binding of ski to be dropped; when ready to drop a ski, shift weight to dominant side single ski; bend knee deeper on single ski for stability; point toe in binding of ski to be dropped; gently slide foot out. *Keep weight on single ski.* Slide foot down along calf to back of the ski, gradually slipping it into back binding. *Do not shift weight onto rear foot until it is in the binding.* Finally, shift weight slightly off front foot to distribute weight equally on both feet.
- Deep-water starts on one ski can be done with back foot in or out of the binding. Body position is crucial: back straight, knees bent, arms straight, and ski at 45-degree angle to water.

INTO THE
SLALOM COURSE

AFTER MASTERING the deep-water start, it's time to move from gently weaving, inside-the-wakes skiing to slalom turning. Even if you never want to run a slalom course, learning to turn properly in both directions and accelerate, or pull through the wakes, will make skiing more fun.

BODY POSITION

Proper body position on a slalom ski is similar to proper body position on two skis. Use your abdominal muscles to hold your back up straight and strong; keep your arms straight with your shoulders rolled back while you ski directly behind the boat. Try to keep your hips in line with the middle point of your feet.

Your back binding should be set so that the toes of your back foot barely touch the rear plate of your front foot. If your feet are too far apart, you can't bend your knees properly, and this keeps you off balance. More important, it makes it more difficult to get the ski to turn. Many skis come with the bindings mounted too far apart, so be sure to do a dry-land check before you take to

the water. When your feet are close together you're centered over the rocker or sweet spot of the ski—the part of the ski designed for holding and distributing your weight.

Turning a water ski is very much like turning a skateboard or surfboard; you use your knees, ankles, and lower body and let the ski do what it is designed for. This is where the back foot comes into play—it is the steering foot.

When you're learning the fundamentals of good turning, it's a good idea to switch from a beginning ski (perhaps half of a combo pair) to an intermediate or more advanced tournament-level slalom ski. The bottom design of a slalom ski allows it to roll from the bottom onto the edge more easily. What I mean by "rolling" is just that: the ski actually rolls onto its side as you turn, enabling you to hold a sharp angle away from the boat or "edge" and to accelerate through the wakes.

As with any new skill, turning and crossing the wake should be practiced slowly, with emphasis on good technique and body position at first.

Adding this new element to your skiing comes almost automatically: you find yourself instinctively beginning to "pull," actually tugging on the line as you edge through the wakes, accelerating as you do so. This is the first feel you will have of proper pulling, which is pulling from the finish of one turn, skiing steadily through both wakes with the ski on a strong edge and going into the start of the next turn. This can be a bit frightening because you begin to accelerate. A common trap skiers fall into is pulling from the turn to the first wake, then letting up between the wakes, skiing on a flat ski, and attempting to put the ski on edge and pull again from the second wake out to the next turn.

To overcome your fear of accelerating through the wakes, concentrate on body position. Keep your eyes up, looking at the horizon. Never look down at your ski or the wakes; remember, if you look down, you fall down. Your back heel should be pressed flat against the ski. Shoulders should be rolled back, and you should be leaning back and away as if you were playing a game of tug-of-war with the boat. If you've ever played this, you

If you learn to maintain good body position from the beginning, you will automatically begin to edge the ski even as you lean away, or leverage yourself against the boat.

know that your upper body leans away from your opponent and your feet are planted firmly between you and your opponent.

These same principles apply to edging and pulling behind the boat. Your upper body leans and twists away from the boat and your ski is leveraged with your legs between you and the boat.

As you start to feel more confident, you'll be leaning away from or bracing against the boat with the ski on its edge. This position helps keep the ski on edge and keeps you from crossing the wake flat, so you slice through the wake, not bounce over it. For competitive skiers, this is one of the most important aspects of slalom skiing because the ski must always be on edge.

Hips should be pushed forward, your behind tucked under, and as you cross the wake, your hands should actually pull down toward your hips as you lean away. This forces the boat to pull from your center of gravity and makes it much easier to maintain proper body position.

A common mistake that many skiers make is bending at the waist causing them to bail out over the front of the ski. Pulling your hands to your hips each time you cross the wake eliminates the chance of this happening.

CAMILLE DUVALL

THE PULL

In order to accelerate through the wakes, you must *pull* on the rope. In one sense, it is actually pulling on the handle, but in another sense it simply goes back to the proper body position I've been emphasizing. Leaning and edging away from the boat constitutes your pull—the harder you lean, the faster you go. It is a myth that a lot of strength is required to edge through the wakes. The pull isn't so much a muscular, physical function as it is a function of proper body position. What you're doing is *leveraging* your body and skiing through the wakes, against the boat. To increase leverage, lean farther away from the boat, not back on the ski; put the ski on a harder edge and push with your legs.

How long should one pull? In free skiing (not in the course), the pull should start the instant you turn your ski perpendicular to the wake or finish your turn. You should continue to pull and edge all the way through both wakes until you feel your ski drop off the second wake; then glide into a change of direction for the next turn.

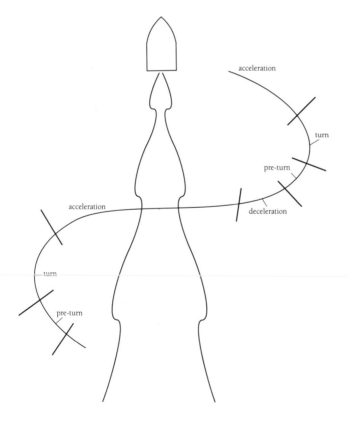

acceleration

turn

pre-turn

acceleration

deceleration

turn

pre-turn

This bird's-eye view identifies each of the phases of the turn. In order to turn properly, you must link all these phases into one smooth motion.

INTO THE SLALOM COURSE

Sometimes this sensation scares people; they feel they're going to fall because they're going so fast and they're not quite in proper body position. They think they'll be pulled over the front of the ski as they start to accelerate.

As long as your back is straight and you're in proper body position with the handle at your hips in the tug-of-war position it's really impossible to fall over the front of the ski. The ski is pushed out in front of you as you brace against it. Practice proper body position on dry land and you'll see what I mean.

A skier can fall over the back of the ski, in which case water often goes where it shouldn't. These falls are a little bit easier on the body than forward falls, but bad body position is still the cause. The contributing factors are the exact opposites of those that cause a front fall; in a backwards fall, the hands are pulled

By practicing on dry land you can get a feel for proper body position: hands low, with the hips up to the handle. This position is very similar to the one used in the tug-of-war position.

Remember, even when you're in the tug-of-war position, you must keep your knees well bent to absorb the shock when you cross the wakes.

up too high, the center of gravity shifts too far back, and the ski slips out from under you. You can also fall backwards if your legs are too stiff. This makes the ski rear up through the wakes; because the ski is not on edge, it becomes uncontrollable. Remember your knees must stay soft and flexible while crossing the wakes. This helps the edge of the ski stay in the water and gives you more control.

It is possible to fall over to one side, away from the boat; this generally happens when the skier drops his head when he leans his body and loses his equilibrium. As your body leans, your head should stay upright, chin and face level with the horizon.

There are plenty of things to think about in progressing from your first deep-water start to cutting back and forth through the wakes successfully. Be assured, you'll take plenty of spills along the way. Some of the falls a slalom skier takes can be pretty spectacular, but they're not always painful. It's wise to remember to signal your driver and observer that you're okay after a fall by clasping your hands together over your head or waving at them. Drivers should hustle back to pick up a skier who has not given the "okay" signal.

Once you've progressed through the pull and learned to cut through the wakes on edge, you'll want to learn how to make smooth, carving turns in preparation for skiing the slalom course. That takes us to our next step.

INTO THE SLALOM COURSE

GOOD AND BAD SIDE TURNS

As you become more adept at turning and pulling through the wakes, you'll realize that you tend to turn harder and more naturally on one side. This has to do with the positioning of your feet in the bindings. If you ski with your right foot forward, turning to the right will be easier and vice versa for left. You can reduce the variance between your two sides by concentrating on body position and keeping your knees flexible. Don't be discouraged if both turns don't feel equally stable at first. Most of the skiers on the pro tour today still have good and bad side turns. Keep working at it; success comes with time on the water.

PERFECT TURNS

I consider the perfect turn one smooth, continuous arcing motion, and don't really like to break it down into components. However, I do think a dissection is helpful for mental visualization purposes in the initial stages of learning.

As you ski from the center of the boat to outside the wake (in whichever direction feels comfortable), you'll go into what is called the "pre-turn" phase. For beginners, this will be 15 to 20 feet outside the wake. When you change the ski from the outside edge (skiing away from the boat) to the inside edge (skiing toward the boat), you're beginning the change of direction. Be sure you move smoothly from one edge to the other, because any hesitation will cause the ski to flatten out and accelerate, making it difficult to turn.

At this stage, both hands should still be on the handle, but the pull of the boat should be felt on the line. Let your arms out smoothly and gradually, reaching toward the boat. This serves two functions: it keeps the line taut and it aids in the rollover or edge change of the ski.

This is where the synergy of the bottom design and bevels of a ski come into play. It is the bottom design that allows the ski to make a smooth transition from one edge to the other. The bevels determine how quickly or slowly the turn can be executed.

When you're in this phase of changing edges, use your back foot to roll the ski from the outside edge to the inside edge. Your

A: Your starting point for a turn should be to edge out from the boat wakes into the deceleration phase.

B: Maintain good body position as you roll your ski from the outside edge to the inside edge. Keep your knees bent, back up, head on line with the horizon; allow the ski to work through the turn. Keep the rope taut by letting it out smoothly and gradually with two hands.

C: As you pull the handle back toward your hips, the ski will finish the turn.

D: You should begin to accelerate at the point the ski finishes the turn and you lean away from the boat.

body weight should be pretty much over the center of the ski, so the ski can do the work for you, even though you will be pushing with your back foot. All of these steps constitute the "pre-turn."

The actual turn is the point at which you kick the back of the ski around, and it is completed when the ski is pointed in the opposite direction. Your knees should be well bent, but you must use them to push the ski around to finish the turn. This is similar to riding a skateboard or surfboard. No ski will turn when the skier's legs are locked straight out. At this stage, with the ski almost around, start to pull your arms down toward your hips. Your head and shoulders should be turned away from the boat and your eyes should be looking 90 degrees away from the boat.

At this point the acceleration phase begins, and you should rock back on the ski into that strong, tug-of-war position for edging through the wakes. Hips should be up to the handle, head and shoulders maintaining the twist away from the boat. This position should be held all the way through both wakes. You'll notice when you watch people ski correctly that when they turn they actually accelerate through the wakes; they *decelerate after* crossing the wakes, as a setup for the next pre-turn.

You decelerate by shifting your weight from the tail of the ski up to the center or the front of the ski. Just as leaning back makes you go faster because the ski tip rises, pushing your knees forward sinks the ski tip into the water, causing it to push more water out of the way, thus slowing it down. A sign of a good skier is someone who can link all four phases together effort-lessly.

ONE-HANDED TURNS

One of the signs of intermediate or advanced skiers is that they can turn with one hand. This sounds much harder than it is. In fact, as you will discover, it's a logical extension of the turning sequence.

If you've ever had some slack rope as you turn back toward the boat, you've turned before the rope is ready or taut. Often, the beginner's style of dealing with slack rope is to raise the handle over his head to take up the slack. This is a very bad habit to develop, and more often than not it results in the handle being pulled from the skier's hand. Although this is a natural reaction to the rope dipping into the water, the best way to get rid of slack line is to do the one-handed turn. Combined with proper decel-eration, and a good pre-turn, a one-handed turn also makes it easier to turn the ski.

To learn one-handed turns, start this way. As you pass from your deceleration stage into the pre-turn, reach across your body toward the boat with both hands on the handle. When both arms are fully extended and you feel the boat pull you onto your inside edge, let go of the handle with the outside hand and gradually extend your inside arm toward the boat. You should still feel some pull. The natural inertia of the boat pulling will make you go from leaning away to a natural edge change that will pull you in toward the boat. During this time the towline should stay taut. You will be using the handle as a pivot point at this stage.

After the ski rolls over or changes edges and starts to come through the turn, grab the handle with your outside hand again and simultaneously pull it down to your hips. Keeping two hands on the handle eliminates the chance of skiing on a flat ski as the ski starts the pre-turn, and most importantly, keeps the line tight during the turn. Remember to "get your hips up to the handle" and concentrate on good tug-of-war body position—the strong-est body position to resist the pull of the boat.

To start a one-handed turn, as you pass from the deceleration stage into the pre-turn, reach across your body toward the boat with both hands on the handle.

As you come to the full extension with both hands, let go of the handle with the outside hand.

Extend your inside hand gradually toward the boat.

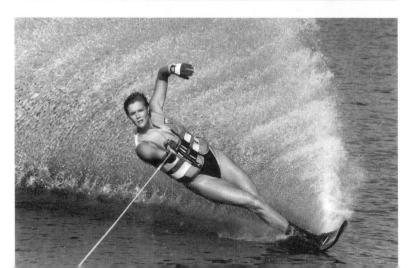

After the ski rolls over, changes edges and starts to come through the turn, grab the handle with your outside hand again.

Pull it in and down toward your hips as the ski finishes the turn.

Lean away from the boat and accelerate.

INTO THE SLALOM COURSE

COMMON PROBLEMS

Timing. As you practice, your timing will get better. Some people let go of the handle too soon, before the ski has gone far enough away from the wake, too early in the deceleration phase. This will jerk the ski from the outside edge to the inside edge. As a result, the skier is forced into a bent-over position against the pull of the boat and the handle is yanked from his hand.

Tendency to over pull. A skier may give one sharp tug just before he lets go of the handle, causing the ski to continue to accelerate. This makes it very difficult for the skier to properly initiate the pre-turn stage because the ski is still going too fast, making it nearly impossible for the skier to turn at an exact point.

Later, this becomes a real problem in the slalom course, because it tends to make the turn too large and looping. The skier will have difficulty getting to the next buoy and will also have a lot of slack line to deal with. It's a good idea to practice until you can turn smoothly on your good and bad sides, putting it all together *before* you attempt the slalom course. You can run an imaginary course, making six turns linked together, focusing on getting one-handed turns down pat, maintaining strong angle through the wakes and good body position.

I see many skiers making a turn on their good sides, then stopping at the wakes and skiing back out to the same side again. This is not an efficient way to practice because the slalom course requires turns on both sides. You must practice turning on both sides in both directions even if they're long, slow turns. Don't worry; they'll get tighter with time on the water and as you mentally replay the proper steps to a perfect turn.

I suggest you think of skiing smoothly from one phase to the other, just linking it all together in a smooth, arcing motion. It's easier on your body and makes more sense to let the ski do the work, and use your body weight for leverage. When you're leveraging against the boat you're using your body weight and larger muscles, the legs and back, rather than just the arms, which can't compare in strength.

Don't muscle it—finesse it. This is actually an easier, stronger and more stable way to ski, and you won't be so sore the next morning. While we're on the subject of sore, you will find that as you increase your aggressiveness and the number of turns, your hands will start to get really sore. You may even develop blisters while wearing gloves. There are a few ways to make your hands more comfortable: you can tape your hands, running the tape lengthwise through your fingers, down to your wrist, and then apply one band of waterproof tape around the injured area. Ice on the hands relieves some of the pain and NuSkin works wonders on open blisters—but it stings. Most of all, keep any open blisters clean and in open air so they'll heal faster.

USING VIDEO TO COMPARE STYLES

One of the best tools we use at our ski school is a video camera. And you don't need to be running the slalom course for it to help you. For example, your observer may offer a style correction, but while you think you've made the correction you still aren't improving. It won't hit home until you see the evidence for yourself. It's especially helpful when everyone who's skiing in your group is a beginner, because it's often difficult at this stage to verbalize changes that need to be made. Take the video home and watch it to see what you're doing wrong and what needs correction. Some boats now provide an outlet into which you can plug your video camera. And most of the newer video cameras have battery packs that are so small and self-contained that you may not even need to go back inside. Compare your body position and style to the photos in this book or the skiers you see on TV. This will help you see where your problems lie.

BEGINNING THE SLALOM COURSE

Exactly what is a slalom course? Once a fisherman who was watching me install a course asked if it was a Martian landing strip. If you've never skied a course, it might look like one. But in reality, the slalom course is a set of six skier buoys, placed in an alternating right-left pattern. Through the center of the six

skier buoys is a set of double buoys designed to mark the boat path.

The accompanying illustration gives a bird's-eye view of a slalom course setup. If you look at the slalom course from the wrong angle, it can look like a bunch of buoys without meaning. But if you look down the length of it, from the boat driver's point of view, everything falls into place. You'll see eight sets of buoys in pairs, all in a line. These are the boat gates. And the six skier buoys will appear on alternating sides of these gates.

For a skier to run the course, the boat must travel at a consistent speed down the center of the boat gates. The skier then rounds each of the six buoys in an alternating, zigzag pattern. (There are also entrance and exit gates for the skier; more on that later.) The challenge of the slalom course is that the skier must turn at an exact point, which never varies. The first time you do it, if you've only free skied before, you'll get a taste of how hard this really is. Basically, it requires the skier to turn on a dime.

I learned to ski the slalom course at age five, and I started competing at age six. I can remember skiing on a slalom course in Lake Hartwell near Anderson, South Carolina. At the time, we didn't have enough money for the tournament-type buoys, which are round and soft, so we substituted rinsed-out Clorox jugs. My most vivid memory of that time is of the bruises that always covered my legs. Often when you turn you'll hit a buoy with your legs, and those Clorox jugs really hurt. Years later, when I went to France to train for the World Championships in Toulouse, memories of that first training site came flooding back. The course in France didn't use Clorox jugs but the type of moorings used for large boats, and they were just as hard as those jugs. Going into the World Championships my legs were covered with bruises from hip to ankle, just as they had been in my very first tournaments. That was the first year I won slalom at the Worlds.

If you have a slalom course with official, tournament-type buoys, you probably won't even notice if you hit them. Still, your ego may be bruised a few times before you conquer the challenge before you.

SLALOM-COURSE TRAINING TIPS

The first time you ever go through the slalom course won't be at the same boat speed or short rope length you see the pros use on TV. Most ski coaches agree that the best way to start the course is with the boat speed relatively slow, generally about 28 mph, depending on the height and weight of the skier. If the skier is a child or a lightweight woman, go a little slower. The actual minimum starting speed in tournaments is 24 mph with a full 75-foot length rope, so I don't recommend starting at less than 24 mph, unless the skier is only five or six years old. Fourteen to 20 mph is a good speed for small children, but the skier will have to know how to start at 24 mph in competition.

There are two schools of thought as to what rope length you should use when first entering the slalom course. The first is that the standard 75-foot rope enables you to get out to the buoys. But at slow speeds, because of the length of the rope, acceleration is practically nil. The second school of thought, which I subscribe to, is to start even beginners on the first loop in a slalom line, which is 15 feet off of a standard 75-foot line. The shorter rope allows a skier to get from one side of the course to the other a little faster. The trade-off is you lose the extra 15 feet of line to help you get around the buoys.

A good driver will help your cause, so it's ideal if your driver

A bird's eye-view of a slalom course. The buoys in the center are the boat guide buoys and the skier entry and exit gates. The six outside buoys are the ones the skier must round.

INTO THE SLALOM COURSE

73

has experience in driving a course. Still, it's not impossible to learn with a less-experienced driver. The driver should aim the boat straight through the middle of the boat gates, and he should be up-to-speed at least 250 to 300 feet before entering the course. When the boat is about 200 feet from the boat gate area, the skier should pull out to the right side of the boat (from his point of view). (If you know anything about running the slalom course, you'll know this is the "wrong" side of the course, but trust me, it's the best way to start out.) The reason I recommend this is that timing for entering the skier gates is critical to the run and most beginners become obsessed with the gates instead of concentrating on the rest of the course. Most coaches recommend skipping the gates and starting on the right side in preparation for rounding the first buoy.

You should concentrate on pulling out so that you're 25 to 30 feet wider than the buoy. When you're 15 to 20 feet from the buoy, start a gentle lean and curve to the left so that you will come as close as possible to the buoy on the down-course side without hitting it.

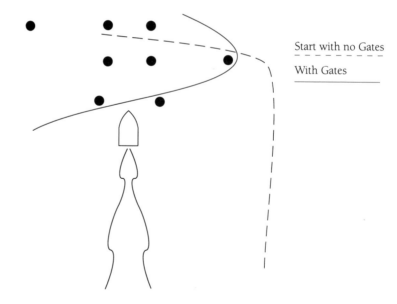

Start with no Gates

With Gates

- - - - - - A beginning skier's path for starting the course without skiing through the gates.
——— The pattern of a skier using the gates to begin the course.

Once you get your ski turned and pointed toward the wake, all your basics of pulling through the wakes properly should come back to you. Get your ski on a 90-degree angle away from the boat, lean into good body position with the ski between you and the boat, shoulders twisted away, pull hips to the handle,

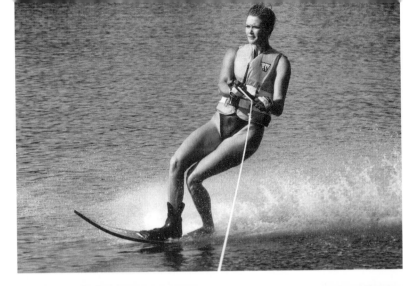

The ski changes smoothly from outside to inside edge at the start of the pre-turn.

The ski finishes the pre-turn and starts to turn back towards the boat. The inside hand reaches toward the boat.

The ski is almost through the turn and the handle is starting to be pulled in to the hips.

The ski is finishing the turn. This is the point of acceleration as the handle comes into the hip and the skier is in the tug-of-war position.

Hard-edge leaning away from the boat. The ski is up between the boat and me, my shoulders are twisted away, the pull is increasing in intensity.

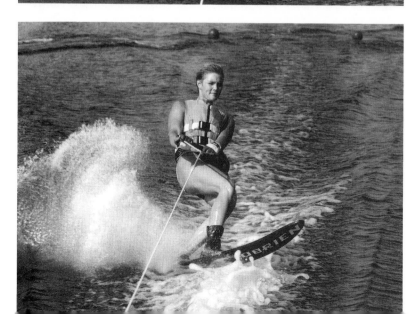

The hardest point of the pull is right behind the boat. Knees are flexible and absorbing the bump of the wake.

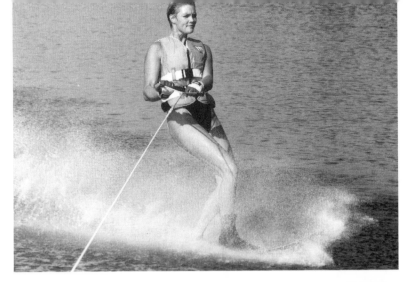

Deceleration phase—start of pre-turn. Ski is in transition from one edge to the other; arms reach toward the boat.

Edge change is complete; initiation stage of the turn.

Arm extended fully toward the boat, ski starting to pivot.

Nearing the end of the turn, reaching for the handle and at the same time pulling the handle in.

Outside hand on handle— nearly the finish of the turn.

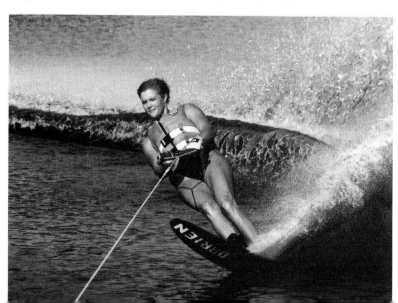

Finish of the turn linking into the acceleration phase.

Acceleration phase—good leverage away from the boat.

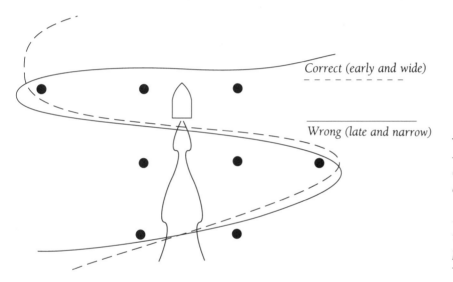

Correct (early and wide)

Wrong (late and narrow)

——————— *correct (early and wide) slalom course pattern*

- - - - - - *wrong (late and narrow) slalom ski course pattern*

handle down, eyes on the horizon directly across the slalom course but not looking for the next buoy. Once you feel your ski drop completely off the second wake, keep your ski on edge for a beat more, start your deceleration phase, and look up for the next buoy. You should be 5 to 15 feet wider than the buoy. Make sure the ski does not go flat; change from one edge straight to the other. Start your pre-turn phase. Repeat these steps over and over until you've rounded all six buoys. Even if you miss a buoy, continue to turn back and forth inside the buoys; it's great practice.

Don't be frustrated if on your first attempt you only get one or two buoys. Even if your style and technique are perfect outside the slalom course, it's very difficult to learn the timing necessary to turn on a specific point. You should, however, remember that you must attempt to stay "early," meaning you must turn as close as possible to each buoy; if you turn farther and farther down the course, you lose ground on the boat and become "late." To stay early, you must really hold your angle and edge and use your knees in the pre-turn. This gives you plenty of time to turn slightly before each buoy rather than at or down course of each. Just keep working with it and eventually you'll be able to run all six buoys.

COMMON MISTAKES

Here are some common errors that almost all skiers new to the slalom course make.

- Not turning close enough to the very first buoy. Don't go 30 or more feet down the slalom course before you actually try to turn; try to turn slightly before the buoy instead of after it.

When you watch top pro skiers you'll see the buoy hit them on their hip or knee or ankle; this is because they're leaning so far in and the rope is so short. This isn't what you should strive for yet, but you should try to turn within 2 or 3 feet of the buoy.

There are only 88 feet, 7 inches between the buoys, so if you've gone 30 to 50 feet past a buoy before you turn, you're going to have a difficult time making up the distance on the other side. Also, remember that keeping that hard 90-degree angle behind the boat is as critical as being close to the buoy.

- The slalom course really shows which side is the skier's bad turning side. Many times when I was teaching at my ski school, if a person's bad side was really bad, I'd keep them out of the course for a few days until we could get their technique smoothed out. You'll only experience frustration if you don't work this out before attempting the course.

For example, if your turn is good at the first buoy, but your turn at the second is bad, it becomes all the more important to practice being early for that number two ball.

Depending upon how much time you actually spend in the slalom course—if, for example, it's just weekends in the summer —it could take you a month or more before you can round all six buoys. If you go to ski school you may manage it, with concentrated effort, in a week or less.

The timing, once again, is critical. Unfortunately, timing is not something that can be taught. It can only be learned through practice, practice, and more practice.

- Another mistake that a lot of skiers make is not skiing way out, wide of the buoy. Being narrow or too close to the buoy makes the skier ski far down course past the buoy. The skier must ski well past the buoy down course to be able to get into proper position to complete the turn. To keep this from happening, make sure you don't begin your deceleration and pre-turn too far inside the line of buoys or too soon. For a professional running on a short line, the deceleration phase is almost on top of the buoys. In the case of beginners, the ski will almost stop as you begin the deceleration phase because the boat speed is so slow.

The pre-turn should be started approximately 5 to 8 feet before the line of the buoy for a beginner; by the time the ski completes a full turn you should be 5 feet or so outside the buoy. Ideally, the ski should already be turned and pointed back at the wake just as the skier passes the buoy. This is the visual image you should strive for.

I know it's very difficult, but you must train yourself not to look at the buoy. It's like driving a car at night. You don't look at headlights because you will tend to drive toward them. The same principle applies to the buoy. If you look at the buoy, you tend to ski right into it, and you'll ski past it before being able to turn. You should try to ski wide and early. The more water you cover before the next buoy, the more space and time you have prior to the buoy for the pre-turn phase. I tell a lot of my students that when they're cutting across the wake, they should look across the lake or behind them over their shoulder. Don't look for the next buoy until you feel the ski drop off the second wake. This habit will apply throughout your skiing career.

Learning to ski wide and early may take a long time. It is often a plateau for skiers to put this concept into practical use, but it is mandatory if you want to ski the course successfully.

THE MINI COURSE—
AN ALTERNATE METHOD

Jack Travers, coach of many world champions, offers another idea for learning the course. He suggests first trying the "mini

The "mini" course
- - - - - - Start with a
narrow pattern around
skier buoys and around
near boat gate.

——————— When you've
mastered that, widen your
pattern around both boat
gates.

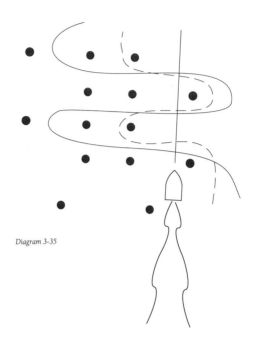

Diagram 3-35

course." To do the mini course, the boat driver steers between the skier buoys and the right side boat gates; in this way, the skier tries to round one set of skier buoys and one set of boat gate buoys.

This is a much easier version of the slalom course because it's not as wide as an official course, yet the same principles for running it apply. When a skier can negotiate the mini course, he should attempt to ski around the far set of boat gate buoys. When a skier can run the full six buoys in this pattern, he's ready to move on to the regulation width course.

GETTING THROUGH THE GATES

Once you've mastered the six buoys on the regulation course, it's time to learn the technique for entering the gates, which can be a frustrating experience until you learn it. If you're consistently rounding all six buoys of the slalom course at 24 to 28 mph, move to this next level.

LEARNING THE GATES

You'll develop your own sense of timing for entering the slalom gates and this will be based on your ski, the water conditions, and your style of skiing.

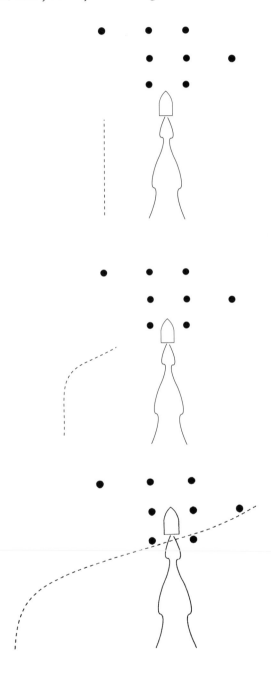

1. Skier path before course, pulling out for the gates.

2. The point at which skier should turn for gates. Note position of the boat in the gates.

3. Skier should strive for as much angle through the gates as possible and to be as near the right-hand gate ball as possible.

The proper path to ski through entry gates to set up wide and early for first buoy.

INTO THE SLALOM COURSE

First, you're going to have to pull out to the left of the boat so you can achieve maximum angle as you cross diagonally through the gates toward the first buoy. My rule of thumb is to make a hard, quick cut to the left, not leaning too far over, using a short, sharp pull when the boat is 200 to 250 feet from the entrance gates. If you look down course, you will be set up in alignment with buoys two, four, and six. At this point your ski should be gliding, not sinking or accelerating.

If you find yourself dragging or sinking, you've pulled out too soon. If you're still accelerating as you reach this alignment with 100 feet or so left before the gates, you've pulled out too late, so adjust accordingly. Let me caution you here about always being able to pull out with the boat in relation to the slalom course. Some people become accustomed to using a particular tree or other landmark at their home site as their reference for when to pull out. If you've been doing this, you're going to have a problem when you go to a tournament at a new site, because your special landmark won't be there.

After you've checked straight ahead to see that you're in alignment with buoys two, four, and six, the next point of reference for you on your right should be the nose of the boat. This sighting is done so you can tell where the boat is in relation to the first set of skier gates (which are orange buoys). You'll have to experiment with your timing, but generally just as the nose of the boat goes through the two buoys, you should put your ski on the right edge and make a smooth, easy, progressive turn to the right increasing leverage as you go, pointing the ski 90 degrees to the boat and aiming wide outside the first buoy. Your hardest pull should be directly behind the boat.

Many first-time skiers become so conscious of making it through the gates that they flatten out the ski coming off a good, hard edge and ski flat to make it through the gates, then try to throw their ski back on edge to be wide enough for the first buoy. This throws off their timing for the whole course. It's absolutely necessary to keep the ski on edge with a 90-degree angle and, even if you miss the gates, stay in proper body position and ski wide and early into the first buoy. If you do this, you'll eventually adjust your timing to get the gates, and you won't ruin the rest of the work you've done on the course in the process. A flat gate with no angle is a guarantee that you won't be able to run the remainder of the course.

Point at which the turn should be executed to go through the gates.

Note the hard pull and edge behind the boat. Knees are well flexed.

Note the proximity to the right-hand buoy and the continuation of angle after the second wake.

As you cross the wakes toward the gates, note where you are in relation to the two gate buoys. If you're on the outside of the course and far away from them, you're too early; let the boat travel farther through the gates before you start your turn. If you're on the inside of both gate buoys, less of the boat should be through the gates when you start your turn, or you'll be late.

To make this process easier:

- Cut down your variables by making sure you're starting from the same width to the left every time, and when you pull out, look down course for the two, four, and six buoys —they should be aligned.
- Make sure you always hold an increasingly progressive edge and work on the timing of your start, with the nose of the boat as a marker, and eventually you'll go through the gates. To give yourself as much advantage as possible, aim to ski as close to the right gate buoy as possible. If you watch pro skiers when they get down to a really short rope, you'll see that 2 or 3 feet in either direction will make a big difference, so where they pass through the gates becomes a critical factor. Timing gates well is a major asset. Just practice and you'll do it!

It's important to keep in mind, when you ski in tournaments, that in order to start your score you must go through the gates at the beginning of the course and out the gates at the end of the course to continue to the next pass.

Your setup for the number-one buoy depends on your timing through the gates. Any good skier will tell you that the gates and number one are the most important part of the course. The rest will fall into place if you get a good start.

MORE COMMON ERRORS

If, as you go through the course, you find that it gets more and more difficult to get outside each buoy, you may be letting up on your pull or not pulling strongly and consistently off each buoy. Sometimes, as you get farther through the course and more excited that you're going to make it, you start to look at the buoys and ski right toward them. If you do this, your run will become too narrow and you'll be skiing farther down course past the buoy. This action makes you later and later, and it becomes harder to get outside each buoy.

I did this myself, when I was trying to set a new world record. At the time, the world record for women was 4 buoys at 38 off of a standard 75-foot line. Before I rounded the fourth buoy to tie the record I was so excited I broke concentration and just looked up too soon. I was pulled in too narrow to turn and fell half a buoy short of the record! Try not to get carried away by the excitement of reaching your goal.

It's a good idea to talk yourself through the course each time you ski it. There's a certain logical progression as you go through: pull, accelerate, decelerate, pre-turn, reach, turn. Talk yourself through each step and as you do you will teach yourself the habit of doing them.

Usually, when you make a mistake in the course and you miss the following buoy, it's because you've left out one of these steps or haven't done it as well as you should have. If you coach yourself through it, you will reduce the problems.

THE NEXT LEVEL—SPEED

Once you consistently make the course—gates and all six buoys—at 28 mph, or whatever your starting speed was, it's time to move on to the next learning phase. In tournament competition, to make things more challenging, the speed is raised in 2-mph increments—from 24 to 26 to 28, successively up to a maximum of 34 mph for women, 36 for men. So wherever you start, if you make the course, bump the speed up 2 mph to increase the level of difficulty, as is done in competition.

By now your boat driver should be able to consistently stay within speed tolerances as well as drive in a straight line. When I train, we always time the boat so that I'm sure I get consistent pulls. To time, the observer should hold the stopwatch (a digital stopwatch is required) in one position. It should be started at the first *boat* gate and stopped at the last boat gate. Keeping the watch in one position, resting on the side of the boat, ensures accuracy.

Don't bump up the boat speed just because you make the pass. Your basic technique will stay with you longer as you progress to higher speeds if you can make each pass consistently, with good form, skiing wide and early, before increasing your speed. That means four out of five times, not one out of five.

Unfortunately, a lot of skiers want to increase their speed as soon as they make a pass. Bumping up the speed too soon causes them to lose their basic technique and develop bad habits that are hard to change later on. So resist the temptation to bump up the boat speed until you're consistent. Of course, if you can easily make the course at 30 mph, you don't need to start at 24 mph every time you go out to ski. You may want to start at 26 or 28 mph, if, and only if, you can make either one the first time, every time with good body position and technique. But do keep in mind that in a competition you have to make your first pass, all six buoys and both gates, in order for your score to get started and continue onward. Starting speed, incidentally, is not an option for pro skiers—women always go 34 mph, men 36 mph.

ADVANCED SLALOM COURSE TECHNIQUES

Remember that as the speed of the boat increases, so does your aggression. By this I mean the strength of your pulls and the angle of your leverage against the pull of the boat. Even though standard ropes are 75 feet in length, a lot of people will begin shortening to the first loop once they start making the buoys. This rope length is called 15 off, meaning 15 feet taken off a 75-foot rope.

Still, even pro skiers who can run very short line lengths, like 35 and 38 off, don't jump off the dock at that short a line length. They start with longer rope, say 22 off, taking a couple of warm-up passes to lock in their technique, get their muscles warmed up, and get their brains focused. For example, when I train, I generally start at 22 or 28 off, which progresses me to the next shortening, 32 off and then shorten to 35 off; all are must-make passes in competition which gives me three to four "warm-up" passes before I get to 38 off, my most difficult pass. In practice, I like to run 35 off twice because mentally it's a difficult pass for me to make in competition. As a beginner trying to build up to proper speed, you should apply this same principle as a progressive building block. Start at an easy pass and work your way up to your hardest pass.

When the rope is the full 75-foot length, you don't have much whip or leverage behind the boat; as you get up to maximum speed, it actually becomes more difficult to make all the buoys because it's harder to accelerate with a long rope. When you chop those 15 feet off the line, you gain a little speed because the distance covered is shorter. It's as though you were on the end of a pendulum or playing crack-the-whip, swinging faster as the line becomes shorter. (If you tie a rock to a string, then raise the rock and let it go, it takes a certain amount of time to rise to the same position on the opposite side. As the rope is shortened, the time it takes to get from one side to the other gets shorter. The same principle applies to shortening the skier's rope from 75 feet—the shorter the rope, the less time it takes for the skier to get from side to side on the course.) This works quite well until the rope length becomes extremely short, and then it becomes difficult just to reach the buoys. Therein lies the trade-off and challenge of the slalom course. The shorter the rope, the faster the acceleration phase. But paradoxically, the deceleration phase becomes that much shorter and must be performed more quickly. Pro skiers have been clocked at short line up to 70 mph during acceleration and down to 20 mph in the pre-turn.

We've talked about bumping up the speed of the boat, and we've discussed the basic principles of shortening the rope. When you shorten the rope length, your technique for getting around all the buoys should remain the same, but your pull and leverage behind the boat needs to be adjusted. You must intensify both. If you're making the 22 off rope length consistently and then go to 28 off, your pull, leverage, and pre-turn have to be a little quicker and more aggressive.

One trick to help you make the transition from loop to loop to shorter rope lengths is to get the driver to slow the boat ½ mph or more as you get into the next line shortening. As you get the feel for the shorter length, the boat can speed back up a little at a time on each pass you complete until you reach your proper speed again. Another technique is to wind several inches of rope around the pylon a few times. This will give you a feel for shorter line lengths without going all the way. I only use this technique if a skier has a mental block when trying a shorter line length.

The chart on page 90 explains what each loop in a slalom rope designates first by overall remaining length of the rope in meters and then by the more common description of the number

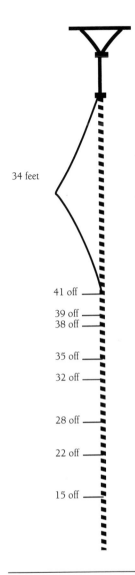

This diagram shows the designated rope lengths for an eight-loop slalom line. The phrase "15 off" means that the rope is 15 feet shorter than its original 75-foot length.

This photo is at 32 off. Note the intensity of angle and aggressive body position.

Note the hard inside edge, tight line, and how much the ski has already turned 10 feet before the buoy.

SLALOM COMPETITION ROPE SHORTENING

1st cut—to an 18.25 meter length (59' 10½" or 15 off)
2nd cut—to a 16 meter length (52' 6" or 22 off)
3rd cut—to a 14.25 meter length (46' 9" or 28 off)
4th cut—to a 13 meter length (42' 7¹³/₁₆" or 32 off)
5th cut—to a 12 meter length (39' 4⁷/₁₆" or 35 off)
6th cut—to an 11.25 meter length (36' 10⁷/₈" or 38 off)
7th cut—to a 10.75 meter length (35' 3¼" or 39½ off)
8th cut—to a 10.25 meter length (33' 7⁹/₁₆" or 41 off)
All subsequent cuts shall be made in .50 meter (19¹¹/₁₆")
  increments.

of feet taken "off" the original 75-foot length. The first method is used to describe rope length in international competition, the second method is the most commonly used method in the United States.

Another training tip is skiing in all wind conditions. Most pro skiers like to ski their hardest pass into the wind, which is an advanced technique that allows you to make up for mistakes by pulling longer and still being able to slow down; the wind in your face actually helps to slow you down at the buoy. In competition, you have the option of starting above the start speed. I recommend you start out easy, with a speed you know you can make. It's a good idea to practice at home, starting at a higher speed or with a shorter rope—it will make you more confident.

Before choosing your starting speed, you may want to check the wind conditions. A few small adjustments can really help you on days when the conditions are less than ideal. Here are some rules of thumb:

- Skiing downwind: Wind pushes your body like a sail, making conditions feel faster

  Keep knees well bent for rough water

  Ski early and wide; it's tough to recover from mistakes downwind

- Skiing upwind: You may want to start your runs so that you have your most difficult run upwind; it feels slower

  Keep knees well bent for rough water

  Pull harder and longer; the wind feels as if it's holding you back

- Cross winds

  Be aware that during your acceleration and deceleration phase the wind will alternately be in your face or at your back so you must adjust accordingly, as per above

It's vital to train in all conditions, not just on perfect days, to get a feel for what each condition is like and to learn how to handle each variable.

Don't be discouraged if you're not ready for the pro tour overnight. Remember, I started running the slalom course when I was five years old. Most of the pros you read about or see on TV have devoted their lives to the sport, so take a hint from us and remember that everything comes with practice, practice, practice. Most of all, enjoy yourself and don't get frustrated when you hit the inevitable plateaus. I also encourage you to use a video camera for analysis, even when you're free skiing. It is a tool that might give you that extra edge, and I'm all for taking any advantage you can create for yourself.

QUICK TIPS

- Break the turn down into phases—deceleration, pre-turn, turn, acceleration—and repeat these steps mentally as you perform them.
- The key to learning to ski the course is to master "edging" through both wakes—riding the ski on its edge instead of crossing the wakes with the ski. Keep your hips pushed forward, your behind tucked under, and as you cross the wakes your hands should pull down toward your hips as your body leans away from the boat.
- Avoid bending at the waist.
- Knees should stay soft and flexible, as shock absorbers, when crossing the wakes.
- To help your bad side turn, really work your legs. The more flexible your knees, the easier it will be for the ski to work and turn properly.
- When you've mastered smooth, arcing two-handed turns, work on learning one-handed turns by letting go of the handle during the pre-turn phase with the outside hand, extending your inside hand gradually toward the boat. As the ski rolls over and begins the turn, grab the handle again with your outside hand and pull it toward your hips as the ski finishes the turn.
- Use video cameras to analyze your skiing.
- The first time you attempt the slalom course, start by setting up wide for the first buoy; ignore the entry gates until you have the timing down on the six skier buoys.
- For beginners in the course, start at a slow boat speed and long line.
- To get a complete turn with maximum angle, avoid looking at the buoys when skiing the course.
- Once you've mastered all six buoys, learn the timing of the gates by gauging your setup in relation to the boat.
- Don't use landmarks for your setup; this will ruin your timing when you ski anywhere other than your home site.

- For easier gate entering, be sure to align yourself with skier buoys 2-4-6 on the left side of the course.
- Don't rush yourself into a faster boat speed. Master proper technique and body position at each speed before moving up. It's vital to ingrain good technique before increasing speed to avoid developing bad habits.
- Practice in all weather/wind conditions if you plan to compete. Tournaments are not always held under perfect conditions.
- Once you are up to maximum speed, begin trying shorter line lengths. Make it easier by reducing the boat speed by about ½ mph when you first attempt a shorter line length.
- Time the driver on each pass. This will increase his accuracy.

FOUR

BOATS AND DRIVERS

OBVIOUSLY, THE MOST IMPORTANT PIECE of equipment a skier needs is a boat. I've seen people ski behind almost anything imaginable, from a 40-foot offshore Cigarette boat to rubber dinghies with a small outboard on the back to the small personal watercraft on the market today. The ideal boat for skiing would be in the 14- to 25-foot range. Competition ski boats are 19 feet long, with enough power to pull a skier easily.

I have a friend who in the late 1970s was an avid skier, nationally ranked in fact. He would have done just about anything to own a ski boat. At the time, however, he was going to college and was on a very tight budget. He managed to scrape together enough cash for a competition ski boat that was about 15 years old when he bought it! He must have found this boat in a junkyard—every part of the boat was blackened with mildew, the windshield was gone, the seats had no stuffing left in them, the gauges were so faded you couldn't read them, and plants had grown up through the floorboards so thickly you needed a machete to drive the boat! To make matters worse, the bilge pump had to be continually running to keep the boat afloat. But the engine was great, and he skied with that boat for many years . . .

although observing for him was an adventure worthy of Indiana Jones!

Many hardcore skiers will go to extraordinary lengths to have the skier's most prized possession: a ski boat. But don't despair; if you already have a boat it can easily be adapted for at least recreational skiing.

UPGRADING YOUR BOAT

The most obvious essential for a good ski boat is adequate power. Some boats simply aren't powerful enough to pull an adult skier out of the water. (If you're only concerned about pulling small children, almost any power will do.)

If you have a stern drive or outboard you may be able to drop the pitch of the propeller, or the diameter or cup of the propeller, to give your boat more low-end acceleration and torque for pulling up adult skiers.

Most boats are designed for top-end performance rather than acceleration, or for a combination of the two. Many boat owners own two propellers, one for top speed and one for skiing. Consult your marine mechanic for advice on sizes to try. It's fairly simple to change a propeller, and an extra propeller doesn't cost a fortune. Plus, you have a spare in case you damage one on a log or by hitting bottom.

The second essential element to a good ski boat is a tow pylon. On competition ski boats the pylon is mounted in the center, ahead of the engine. This makes it easier for the driver to keep the boat in a straight line when a strong slalom skier is crossing back and forth because the pull is from the center of the boat, not the rear.

The ski pylon is mounted on a metal plate under the deck. Having the ski pylon in front of the engine also maximizes the pulling forces involved in skiing.

If a center-mounted pylon is not an option for you, investigate the use of a towing eye mounted on the top center of the transom. Or choose a removable pylon arrangement to suit your boat and engine configuration. Your boat dealer should be able to help you choose an appropriate substitute.

Beware of substituting a lifting ring or tie-down eye on one side of the boat's transom for a skier's tow pylon. It's important

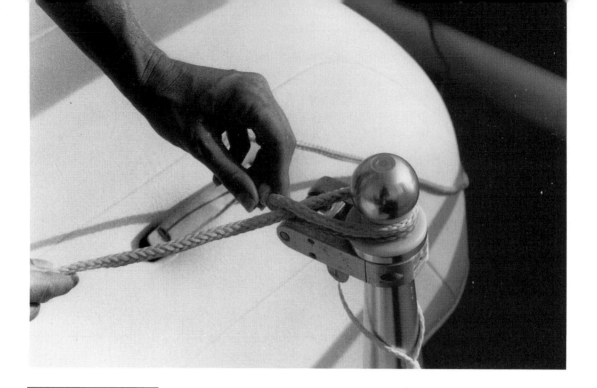

Loop your rope through itself to secure it to your tow pylon.

that the ski rope be attached to the *center* of the boat so that when the skier goes from side to side behind the boat, he can't pull the boat off the preferred, straight-line course. If you attach a ski rope to one side of the boat, it will cause the boat to be off-balance and it will be very difficult to drive.

Most contemporary runabouts have a pair of lifting rings on either side of the transom. If you can't mount a tow pylon or center ski eye, there is one inexpensive solution utilizing these rings. Several companies manufacture a rope or strap bridle that attaches to each ring with scissor hooks or a similar device.

One type has a sliding ring, to which you attach your own ski rope, that slides along the bridle as the skier cuts back and forth across the wake. I prefer bridles with a float in the center, which keeps the bridle out of the prop, and a fixed ring in the center of the bridle. This is the most desirable design, because it gives your ski rope a pivotal point for the pull.

Another component that keeps a good competition ski boat on course is a set of three tracking fins on the bottom. They are mounted in the center of the hull directly underneath the center of the boat to help prevent the boat from sliding laterally when a skier is pulling from side to side. Adding these fins to many boats is impractical and not recommended because if a boat hull is not designed to accommodate fins, it may react unpredictably and dangerously.

Another essential item for a good ski boat is an oversized mirror mounted on the dash so the driver can monitor the skier. In many states, a law requires an observer facing aft; however, other states allow the driver to observe with the help of a rearview mirror.

In recent years, a number of companies have come out with smaller, adjustable side mirrors that clamp onto the windshield frame. As in a car, boat side mirrors are extremely helpful in covering blind spots. The more the driver can see fore and aft, the safer it will be.

Both the ski bridle and extra mirror are inexpensive items easily purchased at a ski shop, boat dealer, marine specialty store, or through mail-order catalogs.

Competition ski boats also come equipped with dual speedometers. These are mounted in the driver's line of vision in case one fails during competition. Accurate speed isn't important until you begin skiing through the slalom course, but if this is an available option you might find it useful to know at what speeds you and your family like to ski. Also, in Florida, as in many other states, we now have speed limits on our lakes and other waterways, so dependable speedometers are a must.

Ideally, the passenger seat should face aft so that an observer can see the skier clearly. Many boats have front passenger seats that swivel and lock in place. If it's an option on the boat you're considering, remember that it's important for safe skiing.

If your boat is a bowrider with a walk-through windshield, it's important to keep passengers out of the driver's line of vision. Ideally, no one should be seated in the bow area when you're pulling a skier, but if they are, be sure they don't sit directly in front of the driver. Aside from these minor adaptations, you should make sure your boat has all the safety equipment aboard required by the U.S. Coast Guard and local jurisdictions, including approved PFDs for everyone.

One other thing to consider the first time you use your boat to pull a water skier: try to distribute the weight evenly on both sides of the boat, especially if you expect to have a crowd aboard. The boat will handle better with the weight distributed evenly, and the skier will have less difficulty crossing the wake of the boat if it's the same on both sides.

All in all, adapting your boat for water skiing is a fairly simple process. And the few changes you make can mean a world of difference in the quality of your skiing.

TOURNAMENT TOWBOATS

I've mentioned tournament ski boats, and I'd like to talk a little more about these specialized inboards. Tournament inboard ski boats have relatively big (usually 350 cubic inches or larger) automotive engines adapted for marine use. The engine sits in the center of the boat because this makes the boat better balanced for planing off quickly and handling and for wake characteristics once the boat's on top of the water. The propulsion system is arranged in such a way that the boat has a lot of torque and power to pull a skier out of the water fast. Often, top speed for these boats is in the 40- to 45-mph range, but most skiers won't need more than 36 mph, and barefoot skiers usually need up to 40 mph maximum. This doesn't seem very fast when you compare it to the speed of a car, but with only your bathing suit between you and the water, it can feel like 90 mph!

Certified tournament ski boats are tested each year by the American Water Ski Association (AWSA) to receive their tournament certification ratings, which are set criteria for power, handling capability, and wake formation. Manufacturers of these boats are very concerned with the shape of the wake their boats create, as they must accommodate not only slalom skiers but also trick skiers, who require a very different performance from a boat. It's no wonder the tournament ski boat is a prized possession of diehard skiing enthusiasts. Fortunately, in recent years manufacturers have begun to accommodate families, so that now a top-flight ski boat can also be an enjoyable family cruiser. If you are serious about your skiing, one of these high-performance machines may well be worth the investment.

THE DRIVER

A boat driver can make or break a skier's performance. A good driver will pull you with a soft touch on the throttle, not slinging you around the turns or yanking you over the front of the ski on takeoff. A good driver won't jerk a young skier out of the water on his deep-water start but pull him up smoothly.

Boat drivers on the pro tour say the best compliment they can receive is if the skier can't tell them anything about their pull. That means the skier didn't notice it and was able to concentrate fully on skiing.

DEEP-WATER STARTS— THE BOAT

Pulling a skier out of the water is very easy with an inboard because these boats have a lot of torque, which allows for a smooth, powerful start to get the skier up. It's important for drivers of inboards to adjust the power to the weight and skill level of the person at the end of the rope. For example, a beginning skier may want to be pulled up slowly and smoothly but not necessarily so slowly that they're being dragged for a long distance. The driver should be careful not to punch the throttle on a beginning skier, as it will undoubtedly yank the skier out of his skis. This is especially true with beginning children and light-weight women. Often they can pop out of the water at 5, 10, or 15 mph, so there's no point in giving them full throttle. The driver must develop a sensitivity to the feel of the throttle.

Of course, if you've got a 300-pound guy with a small slalom ski, you'll need a lot of power to get him out of the water. This is when the driver can punch it and utilize the torque and power of his inboard to get the skier up quickly.

Outboards and stern drives are not usually set up for skiing and may not have enough torque or power to yank a skier up out of the water. This type of setup generally takes a long time to plane off. Because the weight of the engine is in the back of the boat, when power is applied the bow of the boat comes straight up and the stern digs into the water. If you're a skier behind one of these boats it may seem to take an eternity to get your skis or ski planed off. Even if the driver gives it all the power he can, the skier will still have to learn to maintain his starting position while he's being dragged until the boat planes off.

If you have a lot of observers aboard an outboard or a stern drive, try to shift as much weight forward as possible to help the boat plane more quickly. Also, be sure the engine or outdrive is trimmed all the way down into the water for maximum acceleration.

THE WAKES

As a skier, you'll notice a difference in the wakes behind each type of boat. In general, the smaller the better from the skier's perspective. A smaller wake is less challenging to get over, especially for children. Outboards generally have the smallest, flattest wake, but they have a lot of turbulence directly behind the boat. Tournament inboards have a slightly higher, harder wake, but a lot of boat companies have been working on the hull bottom shape of their boats to reduce these wakes, so some are very flat. Stern drives generally have the biggest wakes.

THE PULL

For recreational skiing it's fairly easy to achieve a smooth, steady pull once you've gotten the skier out of the water, no matter what type of boat you drive, if the driver pays close attention. Passengers should communicate what the skier is doing or signaling. Of course, it's always a good idea to check with the skier about what speed he likes before you start. If the skier has no idea, you can adjust according to his hand signals once he's up and going. If the skier doesn't have a feel for the proper speed, an observer or rearview mirror can assist you in finding the right speed. If the skier is sinking in the water, increase the speed until the skis are on a plane. If the ski is slapping the water and the skier is wobbling from side to side, you're probably going too fast.

A good, average speed, depending upon the weight of the skier, would fall somewhere between 20 and 28 mph. If you don't have the luxury of a speedometer in your boat, use the tachometer to gauge the proper speed. It's important for the speed to remain steady, so if you're making adjustments up or down, make them smoothly; the skier can feel every surge of power.

Driving smoothly is not just a matter of adding a little throttle or pulling back a little. As you're driving you should be constantly checking three things—the skier, your speedometers for the correct speed, and all around you for other boats or obstructions in the water. You should be more alert to other traffic than if you were on the freeway, checking the water in all directions around you and your skier, because with no licensing required of boat drivers you have no idea who might be out on the water. And with no defined roads they could come from anywhere.

If you are pulling a heavy skier, or a fairly strong skier, be prepared for the skier to actually pull the boat from side to side, as well as slow it down as he crosses the wakes. This is where skill comes into play, as a driver must learn to add a slight pressure to the throttle as the skier starts his pull. The driver must also learn to work the steering wheel to keep the boat in a straight line. On most inboard boats, this won't be a great challenge.

PATTERN FOR SMOOTH WATER

Most drivers tend to pull skiers around a body of water in large, looping circles. However, as the boat circles it begins to run over its own wakes, which means the skier is constantly battling rough water. The easiest way to prevent this is to drive in what I call the "eye of the needle" pattern.

Optimum driving pattern for smooth water for free skiing.
- - - - - - incorrect pattern
——————— correct pattern

Start off in a straight line parallel to the shore. If the lake is windy, choose the shore where the water is calmest. The driver should pull the skier in a straight line for 30 to 60 seconds. This may seem like very little time, but it's not if you recall that at 34 mph it only takes 16.98 seconds to go through the entire slalom course with the skier making six turns!

When the driver is ready to turn he should signal the skier of his intent, make a smooth turn, and head back down the middle of the path he just made. The wakes the boat created will have dissipated and the skier will have smooth water to ski on.

DRIVING THE COURSE

Learning to pull a skier through the slalom course is comparable to learning to slalom ski. Both take time, practice, and patience.

Most important is learning to maintain the correct boat speed. Of course, your boat's speedometers have to be correct, so you may need to adjust them by using a stopwatch to time yourself through the course. In timing the driver, it's best to have a stopwatch with a lap time on it. If you're the observer, place your hand on the side of the boat and as the entrance gate buoy passes your hand you start the watch. Stop the watch at the third gate buoy of the course, pressing lap time, and note it or tell it to the driver; this will give him some idea how he is doing. You will be timing the boat through the first half of the course and then the total elapsed time at the end of the course as well. This is the way the boat is timed in all competitions to ensure that the speed of the boat is the same for everyone. Note that where you hold the stopwatch can influence the time up to a couple hundredths of a second, so it's important that you leave your hand in the same position on the boat the entire run to ensure accuracy.

In all competitions—pro and amateur—runs are timed and must fall into pre-set tolerances to ensure fairness for all competitors. In professional competition we use automatic timing, which is the most accurate of any method. The system consists of a magnetic plate on the boat wired to a stopwatch, and gate magnetic plates on the buoys. As the two plates pass each other the watch is started, the third buoy time is recorded and then the watch is stopped at the exit gates. All of this information is fed by radio back to the shoreline. We still use a manual timer in pro competition in case the equipment breaks down, because official competition rules state that every run must be timed and fall within the designated tolerance of the correct time. If the boat time is not within tolerance, the skier must run the course again because if the time is too slow the skier has had an unfair advantage over the other competitors. If the time is too fast, running the course was much more difficult than it was for the other skiers. If the skier makes the "hot time" pass he does not have to repeat the run again, but he must rerun the out-of-tolerance slow speed, and if he does not make the run over at the proper speed, he may not continue his score.

It's a good idea to time the driver every time you practice. You'll hardly ever see a pro skier without a stopwatch in his boat. The accuracy of the driver in the slalom course is very important to any good skier, because he needs to know he's running the course in practice within the speed tolerance just as he has to do in tournaments.

Some pro skiers, like my brother, Sammy, are so tuned in that they can actually read the observer's lips when he's telling the driver the time. Sammy's so good at this that to avoid his scrutiny, I always ask the observer just to show the stopwatch to me, so Sammy won't know the time and can't complain if I'm a little off. (He can't yet read the stopwatch while skiing.)

SLALOM TIMES

STANDARD TOLERANCE

SPEED	ACTUAL	TOLERANCE	RECORD CAPABILITY TOLERANCE
mph	seconds		
22	26.33	25.75–26.95	
24	24.14	23.65–24.65	
26	22.28	21.86–22.72	
28	20.69	20.33–21.07	
30	19.31	19.00–19.64	
32	18.11	17.83–18.39	17.89–18.33
34	16.95	16.70–17.20	16.75–17.15
36	16.08	15.88–16.28	15.93–16.23

This chart, from the official tournament rules of the American Water Ski Association, outlines the time it takes, in seconds, for the boat to pass through a slalom course at designated speeds. Because it's difficult for boats to maintain exact speeds when a skier is pulling hard, the "tolerance" times listed are the acceptable range of time for a boat to pass through the course at these designated speeds. The "record capability tolerances" are the designated time for a boat to pass through the slalom course when the skier is skiing for a world record. The tolerances are more stringent for world records to make the speeds as close as possible for all competitors.

This means, for example, if you're going 32 mph, it should take between 17.83 and 18.39 seconds for the boat to pass through the gate buoys. At 34 mph, the range is 16.70 to 17.20 seconds, and at 36 mph it's 15.88 to 16.28 seconds.

Once you get your speedometers calibrated, it will be easier to concentrate on maintaining your speed through the course. Each driver has his own method for achieving correct speed. I allow the speedometer to bounce slightly. For example, if the skier needs to go 36 mph, I might enter the course at 36¼ and allow the speed to bounce down to 35¾ as the skier pulls against the boat. Other drivers set the speed exactly on the line and modulate the throttle to maintain that speed against the pull of the skier. This requires a delicate throttle touch. Practice with both methods and your times will fall within the tolerance.

As for lining up for the course, it's very important to the skier that you are lined up dead center with the driver's gate buoys and moving at a steady speed 300 feet before you enter the course. This can be difficult at such a distance from the course if

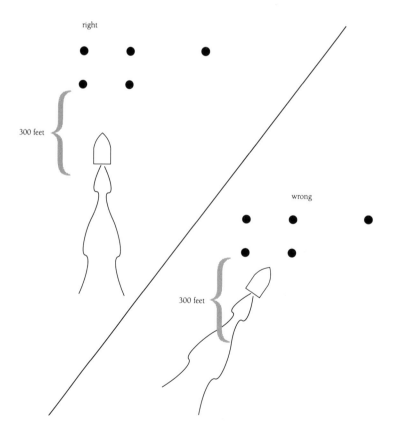

The driver should line up directly with the course at least 300 feet before entering to give the skier ample time to set up.

you have a short turn-around space, but try to line up as quickly as possible. If you always drive the same course, pick a landmark to use as a reference point. When you're actually in the course, it's important to maintain a straight line down the center of the buoys. This can be difficult with a strong skier pulling the boat from side to side. With experience, you'll begin to sense a rhythm and find that just a little pressure on the steering wheel will keep the boat on course. The pull of the skier will be more noticeable on outboards and stern drives, which don't have the tracking ability of an inboard ski boat.

In professional and world-record sanctioned competitions, we use end-course videos. The video camera is lined up on shore on each end, shooting down the center of the course between the boat gate buoys, taping the boat's course through the buoys. If the boat swings more than six inches to either side, the record will be disallowed since this has probably helped the skier through the course, especially when the rope is so short it doesn't reach the buoys. The drivers who work on the professional tour rarely allow the boat to move this much. They are truly skilled and an integral part of the sport.

QUICK TIPS

- Ideally, the rope should be attached in the center of the boat, either in front of the engine on a tow pylon, or with a rope bridle attached on a towing eye to the transom.
- A large mirror mounted on the center of the dashboard and an extra side mirror help the driver observe both the skier and other boating traffic in all directions.
- Evenly distribute weight in the boat to keep wakes level for the skier and to help the driver control the boat.
- Drive with a soft touch on the throttle, pulling the skier up smoothly and gradually. Turn smoothly without increasing speed through a turn.
- To avoid pulling a skier back over your own boat wakes, drive in an "I" pattern, making a loop turn and driving directly down your own path to force wakes and rough water away from the skier's path.

- To drive safely and smoothly, make a habit of checking the skier, your speedometers for correct and consistent speed, and all around you for obstructions or other boats.
- For large, strong skiers, the driver must learn to work the throttle and the steering wheel in synergy to stay in a straight line without jerking the skier or allowing the skier to slow the boat or pull it from side to side.
- Communicate with universal hand signals. The driver should signal the skier his intent to turn by twirling his index finger in a circular motion, and he should warn the skier of bumpy water by moving his hand horizontally in a wavy motion.
- Line up dead center of boat gate buoys and be up to steady speed at least 300 feet before entering the slalom course. This allows the skier time to set up.
- Obtain a copy of slalom course speed tolerances and keep it in the boat with a digital stopwatch. Time the driver each time to increase his accuracy.

FIVE

INSTALLING YOUR OWN SLALOM COURSE

MANY OF MY FRIENDS ask me why I don't freeski without a course. I liken running the slalom course to playing tennis. How much fun would it be just to hit the ball back and forth with no court? It's the same skiing the course. Once you try it you may become so addicted to slalom skiing that you decide you're ready to install a course in your own lake.

Obviously, the first thing you should figure out is whether or not the lake you're considering can physically accommodate a course. While the course itself is 850 feet long, the American Water Ski Association (AWSA) advocates a minimum of about 600 feet of approach space at each end. Therefore, the minimum length required is 2,000 feet. A regulation course, with six skier buoys, end gates, and driver buoys is 75 feet wide, but you'll need at least 100 feet on each side for safety, so a minimum of 275 feet should be available for the width of the course. Add to this state regulations (which vary considerably) of distance from shore, and you may or may not have a site that can accommodate a regulation course.

Assuming your lake or site does meet all these requirements, it's time to get the proper permits. This procedure will vary depending on where you live and how strict local requirements are. If you're applying for a permit on a public lake where boating and water skiing are allowed, there shouldn't be much of a problem. But with the increased boating traffic on lakes all over the country, you can never anticipate what stumbling blocks could be thrown in your way. A good place to start is to investigate the government listings in the blue pages of your phone book. Look for a regional office that sounds like it might deal with waterways. If you can't find one that sounds even remotely possible, try calling your librarian and asking for suggestions.

The American Water Ski Association (AWSA) is always helpful if you run into dead ends, and they will gladly provide you with a wealth of information. Write them at 799 Overlook Drive, SE, Winter Haven, FL 33884-1671.

When I contacted them about background for this chapter, they sent me a huge package of information. Among the many helpful things they sent was a "Legislative Action" package, and a letter from the AWSA public relations manager.

The letter contained the following helpful addresses of agencies that might have jurisdiction over the body of water you'd like to use for your slalom course:

U.S. Coast Guard, 2100 2nd Street SW, Washington, DC 20593; 202-267-2267. (Ask for the office of Navigation Safety and Waterways Services.)

U.S. Army Corps of Engineers, 200 Massachusetts Avenue NW, Washington, DC 20314; 202-272-0010. (Ask for the Office of Public Affairs.)

Federal Bureau of Land Management, U.S. Department of the Interior, 18 and C Streets NW, Washington, DC 20240; 202-343-9435. (Ask for the Department of Public Affairs.)

Federal Bureau of Land Reclamation, U.S. Department of the Interior, Bldg. 67, Denver Federal Center, Denver, CO 80225; 303-236-7000. (Office of Public Affairs.)

National Park Service, U.S. Department of the Interior, P.O. Box 37127, Washington, DC 20012; 202-343-6843. (Office of Public Affairs.)

These agencies will refer you to the appropriate regional office. You might also contact your State Boating Law Administrator for what steps should be taken to grant access and allow installation of slalom courses.

If you run up against potential legislative action to restrict slalom courses, you'll want AWSA's legislative action outline. AWSA will provide all possible assistance.

You should consider forming a water ski club under AWSA. Sometimes, if you meet with local resistance, there is strength in numbers. If you're not a member of AWSA, I strongly recommend you join, as they offer a wealth of information and benefits for skiers and ski clubs, including insurance for members.

INSTALLING THE COURSE

Let's say you've got the site, and you've gotten permission. Now you're ready to jump right in and install the course. Here are a few hints to make the job run smoothly.

First, installing a slalom course is a day-long procedure—*if* you start early in the morning *and* you have several helpers. Don't try to do it yourself—it's just not feasible.

Second, your job will be much easier if you have all your equipment in order. Also, it's vital that you have a boat and a good boat driver, since he'll play a key role. Most of the things I'll be warning you about in this chapter I've done wrong at one time or another myself. So trust me when I tell you it's a lot easier to get organized *before* you get out on the water.

EQUIPMENT

There are some basic ingredients you'll need for your course. There are twenty-two buoys—ten safety orange (six skier buoys plus the entrance and exit gates), and twelve safety yellow for boat gates. If you're on a budget, you can substitute antifreeze jugs and Clorox bottles (provided, of course, you clean them thoroughly first so you don't pollute the lake). I don't recommend milk jugs for the boat gates because they tend to break apart easily and sink. If you're not on a budget, I'd suggest buying buoys from AWSA or through one of the mail-order waterski warehouses. As long as you're placing the order, you might as well get a few extras of each color to have on hand for replacements.

In addition to the main buoys, depending upon the method you choose for anchoring, you may also need twenty-two sub-buoys. In Florida, because of murky water, we like to use the small, six-inch Styrofoam lobster trap buoys, but you may also use Clorox bottles stuffed with Styrofoam. Whatever you use, it's a good idea to paint them a fluorescent color so you can locate them when necessary.

If you're installing the course on a public lake, you may wish to use snaps and surgical tubing or slices of inner tubes to make rubber bands for your main buoys; this way you can remove your course when your club isn't using it. (This also keeps down the cost of replacing buoys.)

You'll need plenty of rope to tie the buoys to the anchors. The best choice is quarter-inch polypropylene line because it doesn't rot, stretch, or shrink. The amount of line you use will depend on the anchoring method you choose, the depth of the water, and the amount of water-level fluctuation. If you're putting your course in a spring-fed lake with little or no variation in water level, you should plan to set your anchors with sub-buoys about 4 feet below the surface so they won't get torn out by passing boats. You'll need enough line to accommodate this depth and enough inner tube and surgical or spear gun tubing to stretch from the sub-buoy to the surface buoy.

There are three main methods of anchoring buoys, and the rest of your equipment depends on which you choose. The most common method is to use one or two concrete blocks, depending upon the consistency of the bottom. If it's muddy or mucky and the block will settle, one may be enough. If it's hard or sandy, you may need two strapped together, or even need to fill the holes of the blocks with extra concrete. (Be sure to put newspaper underneath the holes when you pour the concrete so it won't run out.) For more permanent anchoring, screw anchors or metal stakes driven into the bottom may be used. The anchors that you use are quite important; if they are not heavy enough they will shift or be pulled out of alignment by a passing boat, which alters the measurement of your course.

In some areas, where water level varies a lot, it may be necessary to use a counterweight system for each buoy to keep the anchor line tight.

Keep in mind that it's better to splice your line than knot it, because the knots come undone easily. Also, if your line is going to be through or around a concrete block, you'll need to thread it through some sort of tubing to prevent chafing. (An old garden

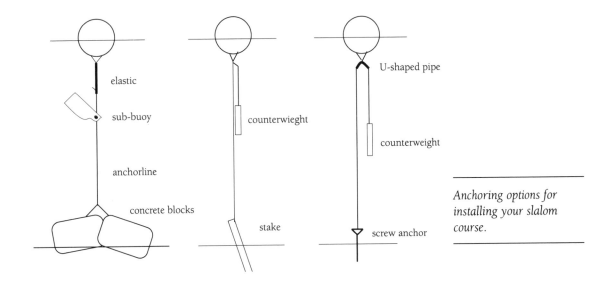

Anchoring options for installing your slalom course.

hose can do, or you can buy special tubing for this purpose.) I always recommend purchasing more line and tubing than you think you'll need, to allow for mistakes.

A couple of extra items that experience has taught me are mandatory to have along include utility scissors, two-way radios, swim fins, a wetsuit, a bicycle pump, and a basketball needle.

Utility scissors are easier to use than a knife, and if you tie them to some extra line and then tie that line to a buoy, you can keep them handy in the water and not worry about losing them. You'll need a bicycle pump and basketball needle to inflate your buoys when they deflate. While you're at it, inflate a couple of extra buoys and throw them, as well as some extra straps, under the bow of your boat; you'll be prepared whenever you go to ski and find a buoy missing from the course. Radios are good if you're working with a professional surveyor, which we'll touch on later. And whoever is in the water will last much longer if he uses swimfins and wears a wetsuit—even in the summer. You'll be in the water a long time, and there's no point in risking hypothermia. Life jackets will help prevent fatigue but can't be used when diving.

SETTING UP

The most difficult part of setting a slalom course is determining where your buoys will go. All world record capability courses and those used on the pro tour are set up by professional surveyors who use a theodolite to ensure accuracy. The surveyor actually measures your shoreline first, then determines where the course will go in relation to it.

It is, however, not necessary to hire a professional surveyor to install your slalom course. The AWSA recommends the use of a large, wooden square for easy, warm-weather installation. (I'm not even going to discuss cold weather installation. It seems to me you should be doing something else if your lake is frozen!)

Official Slalom Course

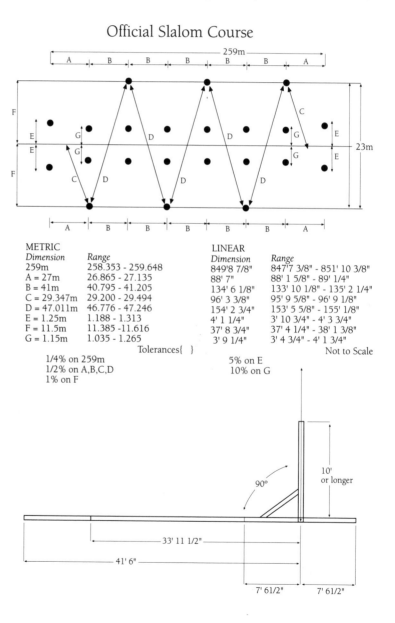

METRIC		LINEAR	
Dimension	Range	Dimension	Range
259m	258.353 - 259.648	849'8 7/8"	847'7 3/8" - 851' 10 3/8"
A = 27m	26.865 - 27.135	88' 7"	88' 1 5/8" - 89' 1/4"
B = 41m	40.795 - 41.205	134' 6 1/8"	133' 10 1/8" - 135' 2 1/4"
C = 29.347m	29.200 - 29.494	96' 3 3/8"	95' 9 5/8" - 96' 9 1/8"
D = 47.011m	46.776 - 47.246	154' 2 3/4"	153' 5 5/8" - 155' 1/8"
E = 1.25m	1.188 - 1.313	4' 1 1/4"	3' 10 3/4" - 4' 3 3/4"
F = 11.5m	11.385 -11.616	37' 8 3/4"	37' 4 1/4" - 38' 1 3/8"
G = 1.15m	1.035 - 1.265	3' 9 1/4"	3' 4 3/4" - 4' 1 3/4"

Tolerances{ }

1/4% on 259m
1/2% on A,B,C,D
1% on F

5% on E
10% on G

Not to Scale

If you decide to use the large wooden square method of positioning the skier buoys, here is the way to construct the square.

90°

10'
or longer

33' 11 1/2"

41' 6"

7' 61/2"   7' 61/2"

The square, as illustrated, can be made of straight two-by-fours bolted together with marks painted at the specified measuring points. A rope extension will help in positioning the square when it is in use.

First, anchor a buoy at one end of the course. Next, temporarily anchor a buoy approximately where the opposite end of the course should be. This will establish your directional line. Work from the first buoy and measure the distance from one buoy to the next by using premeasured lengths of rope. By sighting down the row of buoys, an observer in the boat can communicate to the swimmers where to position the buoys.

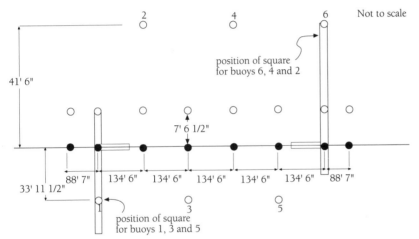

Putting the square to use for buoys #1 and #6.

According to instructions offered by AWSA, your first line of buoys should be boat guide buoys. They can then serve as references for the square you built. The square will be used to determine the correct perpendicular distance out to the skier buoys and the second line of boat guide buoys. See the illustration for positioning the square to determine placement of skier buoys one, three, and five. Align the short arm of the square with your line of buoys. (A swimmer can hold the rope extension with a slight tension at the next buoy in line for a more accurate reading.) When the long arm of the square is perpendicular to the line of buoys, anchor the skier guide buoy at the 33-foot-11½-inch mark and the other boat guide buoy at the short end. Repeat this procedure for skier buoys three and five. The purpose of measuring three areas at once is to keep the buoys the correct distance from each other as well as at the correct width.

To install skier buoys six, four, and two on the other side of the course, use your original line of eight boat guide buoys. When the square is in perpendicular position for skier buoy number six, anchor buoys at the 41-foot-6-inch mark and the 7-foot-6½-inch mark. Repeat to install the last two skier buoys. Visually check all buoys to be sure they are aligned.

Finally, the end gate buoys are supposed to be 8 inches farther apart than the course guide buoys, so move each out 4 inches and you'll have a regulation course.

OPTIONS

If this sounds like more effort than you'd like to put into a slalom course, there are "portable" courses available, such as the Accufloat. There are both advantages and disadvantages to portable courses.

First, these courses are usually made of PVC pipe in a skeletonlike configuration that is connected with thin wire. They are good if you have a very deep lake or if you have a lot of movement in the depth of the water. They *can* be moved, although it's not as easy a task as one might think.

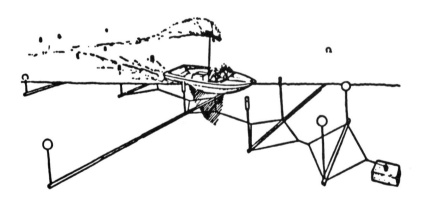

An underwater view of a portable slalom course. Note how the buoys are anchored to a "spine."

By and large, portable courses are weighted only at either end. The accuracy of the course depends on the tension kept between buoys. Therefore, you must get the line from the "spine" to the buoys exactly the same length. If not, the spine can bow and throw your course totally out of whack. Also, once such a course has been in for a while, the PVC tends to attract algae and slime. The resulting added weight can make the spine bow or sink, making your course too narrow or easy. Even strong wind can make the spine bow, giving you a shorter, harder course. Also salt water can rust the connecting wires.

The main advantage to such a course is that it's portable and prepackaged. And it requires installing only *two* anchors rather than twenty-two. I used one myself at my ski site in the Bahamas until we had time to install a permanent regulation course.

CAVEATS

First, before you get out on the water, put everything you'll need in the boat. You'll save a lot of time and frustration if you premeasure and precut your line. In addition, you may wish to add a bit of tape with the distance written on the precut line for accuracy. Attach the surgical tubing to the buoys (and snaps if you need them), and also attach the line separately to the anchors. You'll need to make adjustments in the water for depth, so don't rig the entire thing.

A boat with a swim platform is a real energy saver. To protect your platform against the ravages of concrete blocks, put a piece of plywood over it.

If the water where you're installing your course is very deep (over 10 feet) and you'll be moving up and down a lot, consider enlisting the aid of a certified scuba diver. Surface swimmers can help with fine tuning, but going up and down as often as you'll need to for setting all these buoys can be exhausting.

When cutting inner tube or surgical tubing, cut the ends in a pointed shape. This will go through the buoys more easily. A piece of plastic pen or a rope fid makes a good guide for line or tubing to go through a small, sub-buoy.

Make sure you have a good boat driver because he does most of the shuttling of equipment and, if he's on the ball, anticipates your needs. A good boat driver will make the whole project go more smoothly.

Finally, be courteous to other boaters, especially on public lakes. If a fisherman is enjoying his sport nearby, let him know that you are using the course and not intentionally trying to scare away fish. Nine times out of ten he will appreciate your courtesy and will probably move, or at least not throw his fish hook your way when you ski by. Everybody can enjoy the lake together if you use common courtesy and common sense.

In addition, your ski club can score points by offering ski clinics and free ski safety seminars. A ski club–sponsored lake clean-up is another way to score points with the public. And with the ever-increasing popularity of boating, it's important to re-member boaters have just as much right to be there as you. Who knows, you might just enlist a new fan of the sport.

QUICK TIPS:

- Handle any legal issue before you start.
- **Slalom course installation supply list**
slalom course diagram measurements
10 safety orange buoys
12 safety yellow buoys
22 sub-buoys
spool of ¼-inch polypropylene line
surgical tubing
concrete blocks, screw anchors, or metal stakes
snaps
utility scissors
two-way radios
swim fins
bicycle pump and basketball needle
wetsuit
extra life jackets
plastic pen or rope fid

Be sure you have it all before you go!

COMPETITIVE
JUMPING

JUMPING IS ONE of the most thrilling disciplines in water skiing. It's a go-for-broke event where the longest jump wins. It's known as a daredevil event on the pro tour because skiers are flying through the air distances of more than 200 feet—two-thirds of a football field—at over 70 mph. Yet it doesn't really have to be so dangerous until the professional level. It all depends on the amount of ability and guts you have and in what mix.

The equipment is high tech and specialized. Most of it is extra safety equipment. The first and most obvious need, though, is a pair of jump skis. Not just any skis will do. Jump skis are as different from slalom skis as night and day. They are rather blunt-looking when compared to a slalom ski and about 6 inches wide, with a slight narrowing under the bindings. The skis are broad and flat, with no bottom shape and no bevel or side cut—the sides are square and sharp. They turn up much more on the tips than a slalom ski does, and they have minimal rocker.

The fins on the bottom of jump skis are long and flat, as opposed to the deep, short fins found on slalom skis. A jump fin is about 10 inches long, very pointed and streamlined—like a bullet on the front—and only about 1½ inches in depth. The backs of some skis are a dog-bone shape, not rounded or squared

off but indented in the middle. Some are square and others are rounded, but all are softly shaped. The shape of the tail controls the path of the water, and a smooth water flow will make the ski go faster.

The technology for jump skis is constantly changing because pros are always searching for that extra edge to add a few feet to their jumps. What you look for in a pair of skis will depend on your jumping ability. The skis themselves are made by compression molding and are fairly stiff; generally they have graphite inside for extra stiffness. The skis have some flex in them because they must absorb some of the shock of your landing, as well as the shock of leaving the water and hitting the jump ramp surface. A material called ABS plastic is used for the top and bottom, which seems to be the slickest product to use with the surface of jump ramps. Jump skis also differ from slalom skis in that they have a rubber edge all the way around the skis to protect the skier from the sharp edges.

Production of jump skis is labor-intensive, and high-tech research is costly. Coupled with the low volume of sales, jump skis are very expensive, anywhere from $400 to $1,000, depending upon the type of bindings you purchase with them. But since jump skis must withstand the impact of hitting a jump ramp at over 70 mph and a drop to the water equivalent to jumping off a two-story building, I for one want the finest materials money can buy attached to my feet.

Jumping requires a lot of specialized gear, including a helmet, an arm sling, a flotation wetsuit, a good pair of jump skis, gloves, and, of course, a rope.

In addition to a good pair of skis, jumpers need a specially designed wetsuit, which has extra padding in the rear-end area so water doesn't go where it's not supposed to. Most jump suits are made with extra flotation built in, so you don't have to wear a life vest and are more aerodynamic for pushing the 200-foot barrier (which is 5 feet shy of the men's world record, held by my brother). The padding is also good protection against injuries.

Another required piece of safety equipment for AWSA tournaments as well as internationally sanctioned tournaments is a jumping helmet. There are helmets specifically designed for water skiing, but I've seen skiers use all types, from hockey helmets to bicycle helmets to polo helmets.

While a helmet should protect you while you go over the ramp, it should snap on the side so that the force of the water can blow it off if you have a bad landing. It's not uncommon for jumpers to injure their necks when landing as the water rushes up and whiplashes the helmet.

My experience in the 1986 Masters tournament is a good example of why a helmet should blow off. In Saturday's preliminary rounds, on my second jump out of three, I had a very late cut to the ramp. Thinking I would hit the side of the ramp, I sat back as my skis went onto the ramp. Almost crashing, I fell backward on my skis and slapped the water hard. I landed very far back and the snaps on my helmet were so rusty that they didn't pop open. The force of the water caused my helmet to bucket and water rushed through the helmet; as the force of the water was relieved the helmet whiplashed my neck and slammed my head forward, bouncing the helmet—and my head—into the tips of my skis. I bit my tongue and I came up spitting blood everywhere. Because my first jump was not long enough to make it to the finals, I was under a lot of pressure to make a really long jump on my third and final attempt. Fortunately, I was able to come back and do it despite the disaster. It just so happened a reporter from *Sports Illustrated* was there to cover my brother Sammy and me at the Masters. What terrible timing for a freak accident!

An optional piece of equipment most jumpers use is an arm sling, but it's not something a beginner will need. An arm sling is a wide-webbed belt that fits around the skier's lower abdomen or hip area and has a loop into which the skier's right arm fits; this keeps the arm tucked into the body. The purpose of the sling is to help maintain proper body position by pulling the hips forward as the skier gains speed and momentum on the approach to the jump ramp. It's worn on the right side because if worn on the left arm it would cause you to spin toward the boat in midair due to the direction of your cut to the ramp.

A good rule of thumb is that if you can jump 100 feet on a 5-foot ramp at 30 mph, you're ready to begin using an arm sling.

The rope used for jumping is a standard 70-foot length with a 5-foot handle.

The final piece of equipment that will make a huge difference is a good pair of gloves to help you hold on to the handle as well as prevent blisters.

JUMP RAMP

The main piece of equipment is the jump ramp itself. It is a floating platform 21 feet long, from the waterline to its highest point, and 14 feet wide. The surface is usually made out of a fiberglass-type material, similar to the hull of a boat, with perhaps a little texture to it. Ramps can be any color, but they are usually bright safety orange. Most ramps have a system that allows water to trickle down over the surface so that it stays wet, and it may or may not have some type of paraffin wax on it, which helps skiers slide across the surface a little faster. On the sides of the jump ramp are safety curtains or aprons to protect skiers from skiing underneath the superstructure of the ramp.

The supporting structure is generally made out of a lightweight I-beam steel, but it can also be made out of wood. The ramp is generally floated on long billets of Styrofoam, like those seen under floating docks, or barrels. Of course, the ramp will be anchored to the bottom so that it doesn't move, and this requires heavy weights.

Official Jump Course

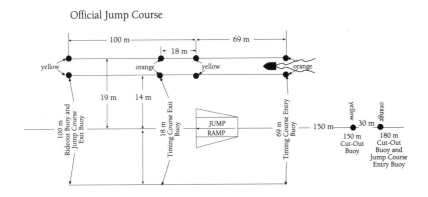

Set up along the right side of the jump ramp is a course similar to a slalom course, with boat gates and skier buoys. Years ago, skiers had the option of jumping from the right or left side (we called it "Texas style" when skiers jumped from the left), but most people preferred the right-hand side so the option has been eliminated. Everyone now jumps from the right.

The angle of the jump ramp is adjustable—by angle I mean the angle of the ramp surface, which is the height of the jump ramp from its highest point to the water level. Most people jump on a 5-foot ramp. (Women, including professionals, always jump on a 5-foot ramp.) The only exceptions, in competition, are the Men's I division, Men's II, and Open Men. These jump with it set at 5½ feet, and if you meet a set performance standard you have the option of jumping on a 6-foot ramp (in Open division only), which is the height pro men jump.

The 6-foot ramp has been likened by men jumpers to hitting a wall at 70 mph. And many pros have had career-ending injuries from crashes off a 6-foot ramp.

Depending on your age group, water-ski federations have set maximum boat speeds for safety reasons. These range from 28 mph for the youngest skiers to 32 mph for pro women, up to 35 mph for professional men. The concept is: the faster the boat goes, the more speed a skier can generate, the farther he can jump. The catch is: the faster the boat goes, the harder the fall.

This accounts, in part, for the disparity you'll see between men's and women's scores in pro events on TV. Women on a 5-foot ramp going 32 mph generally jump in the 140-foot range. Men on a 6-foot ramp at 35 mph have scores in the 185 to 190 range. That extra foot of height and extra speed can make a 50-foot difference in distance. As of this writing, the jump record for women is 156 feet and the men's is 205 feet, held by my brother, Sammy.

COMPETITION

Jumping in competition requires supreme concentration and courage. The best example of this that I can think of is from a World Championship tournament in 1987. My brother, Sammy, was skiing for an unprecedented fourth World Overall title. Since the World Championships are only held every two years, this represented his domination of the sport in all three events for eight years.

He hadn't skied well in slalom and he'd fallen early in tricks, so his title depended upon the outcome of the final event: jumping—his specialty. To add to the pressure, because his next closest competitor was performing very well, Sammy was going to have to jump 199 feet behind an inboard—something that had never been done before in competition. (At the time, the world

My brother Sammy Duvall, world-record holder at 205 feet in the Men's Jump, on his way to another 200-foot Tournament victory.

record was 202 feet, set behind an outboard.) On top of this, just before he skied, there was a tense altercation on the starting dock with another competitor's father who was deliberately trying to unnerve Sammy. A lesser skier might have allowed it to break his concentration. Sammy, however, channeled all his adrenaline into a record-setting 200-foot jump and his fourth World Overall title.

COMPETITION RULES

The skier gets three tries at the jump ramp and the single longest jump is his score. One of the questions I get asked most often is how jumps are measured in competition. It's done by a computer triangulation system from shore. Three metering stations are set up strategically from the ramp and there are two judges on each.

The judges look down a sighting arm (similar to a gunsight) that is attached to a protractor mounted on a stand. As the skier lands, a plume of water shoots straight up like a geyser. Each judge sights in on the plume; the readings of the two judges' protractors are averaged, and this information is fed into a computer that triangulates the distance and position the skier landed in relation to the ramp. The exact point the skier landed is not how competition is scored, but this indicates the accuracy of the system.

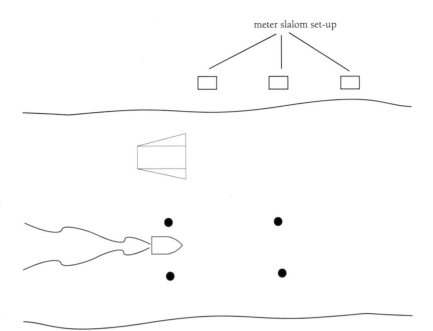

meter slalom set-up

This bird's-eye view of the jump course shows the location of the three meter stands used to measure distance in relation to the jump.

For a skier to receive a scoring jump he has to ski past a ride-out buoy 100 meters from the front of the jump. When you're skiing in competition, it's a big advantage to know the distance you've jumped, so you can make adjustments to your approach to the ramp. As you ski back down the lake to set up for the next jump, the scorer will radio your distance to the boat, and the judge in the boat will relay the information to you with hand signals. At the pro tour events we have a scoreboard for the crowd similar to the type used at football games; it's great to be able to see your distance as you ski by. With computers, the distance is flashed on the board almost before the skier skis away.

Before scoreboards came into use, skiers relied solely on the judges in the boat to learn their scores. In Europe, it can be confusing for Americans because the score is given in meters. So we developed a system for the judges to tell us from the boat. For example, if you jumped 140 feet, the judge would hold up one finger, then four fingers, then a balled fist—one, four, oh. Last summer when I competed in London at a pro tour stop, we had a judge from England in the boat. She didn't quite understand the system and when she attempted to tell me my score she would hold up ten fingers at a time. Needless to say, although she was trying to be helpful, it was a little difficult to add up all those fingers!

WHEN YOU'RE READY TO TAKE THE PLUNGE

The key ingredient to being ready to jump is desire. When I was seven-years-old and my brother was five, my father tried to figure out a way to motivate us to try jumping. Like any father, he resorted to bribery. We'd get twenty-five cents for any jump we skied away from. I really didn't want to jump and no amount of money was going to change my mind. Sammy, however, felt this was a much easier way to make money than by doing chores. So he made lots of money jumping that summer—and every summer since.

You are ready to try the jump if you're proficient at skiing on two skis, crossing the wakes comfortably, and in control with great body position. While you can certainly use this book for reference, if you're serious about learning to jump, it's best to go to a ski school. Not only will you have a professional teacher, but they'll have all the specialized equipment there for you to use and try. If you really like jumping, then you can purchase what you need.

TEACHING TECHNIQUES

Coaches use one of two techniques to take a skier over the ramp the first time. Some coaches will take the skier in a straight line directly over the top of the ramp the first time out. Others will use an approach in which you use only a small portion of the ramp.

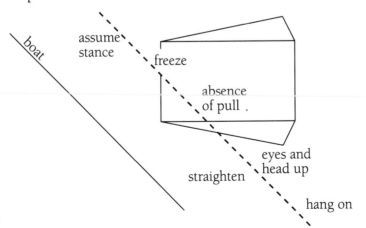

The boat and skier path for riding over the side of the ramp for a first-time jumper.

I prefer to use the second technique when I teach someone to jump (see illustration). I believe it's less frightening for the skier to go over only a portion of the ramp the first time out. Also, the skis won't be on the surface of the jump ramp very long. The skier will only go over 7 to 10 feet, rather than the full 21-foot length. This enables him to become accustomed to the feel of the skis on the ramp in small doses.

Many people expect the ramp to feel slow or sticky, but actually it's like a piece of greased ice compared to the surface of the water. So in going over a portion of the ramp, you minimize that feeling of slickness and become accustomed to the sound and feel of the skis on the surface and the sensation of flying through the air even if it's only for a few feet.

When you go over the corner of the jump ramp, the boat won't be going in a straight line beside the ramp. The driver will swing to the far left side of the ramp, then turn and head toward the ramp at an angle, passing the ramp on the right close enough so that all the skier has to do is go over the left side of the wake and they'll go over the bottom right corner of the ramp. The path will be different when you are ready to go over the top of the ramp. Since jumping can be dangerous, it's vital to have an experienced driver.

The mainstay for a beginning jumper is body position. Proper body position is with feet shoulder-width apart, knees pushed forward, weight on the balls of your feet so that your hips try to fall into alignment with your ankles. As always, your back should be straight and strong. The arms shouldn't be all the way out, nor should they be tucked into the chest. If your elbows are touching your life vest or wetsuit, your arms are in the right position. Eyes should be on the horizon.

Jumping is where the old warning "if you look down, you fall down" really comes into play. It's not necessary to look down. The water will still be there. If you look down the tips of your skis tend to point down, which makes for a nasty face plant.

Skiers who have the most success in making it over the jump ramp the first few times are the ones who get into the proper body position, lock it in, and don't alter it no matter what the surface of the ramp feels like.

The most common mistake made by new jumpers is when their skis touch the slippery surface of the ramp and they pull back on the handle. The skis then go out from under them and

Proper body position for jumping is with your feet shoulder-width apart, knees pushed forward, weight on the balls of your feet so that your hips try to fall into alignment with your ankles.

the skier falls backwards. It's the same effect as pulling back on the rope when trying to get out of the water.

OVER THE TOP

Once you've successfully made it over the side of the ramp with good body position a few times, even if it's just your first

A

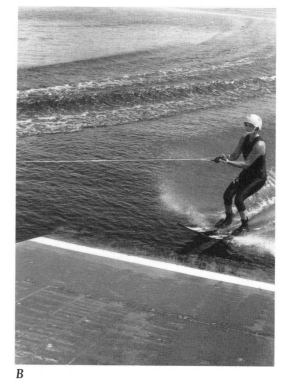

B

A: Approach the ramp on the left side of the boat wakes in proper position well before the ramp.

B: The body position remains constant. Note the small area of ramp to ski over.

C: Maintain proper form especially on the surface (this is where the start of most falls occur).

C

set, you may be ready to go over the top. Allow your jump coach to be the judge.

As mentioned earlier, the boat path will be different when you go over the top of the ramp. For this, the boat will pass by the right side of the ramp, generally going 20 to 25 mph in initial sessions and within 10 to 15 feet of the ramp. The driver won't use the boat path of buoys but will instead drive very close to the ramp. The skier should pull out to the left side of the wake, setting up a little wider than the jump ramp, at about 200 feet before the jump.

Don't worry about missing the ramp because once you've swung out wider than the ramp the boat will pull you back to center. Once you're out to the left, lock down into the proper body position and keep your eyes glued to the top of the ramp. Don't worry about where you come on to the bottom of the ramp because at this point it won't make any difference. Very rarely will you go straight up the center. More than likely, you'll hit the ramp on the left side, ski diagonally across it, and come off the top-right corner.

D: Eyes up, tips slightly up, maintain good position.

E: Still frozen in position for landing.

D

E

skier

When learning to go over the top of the ramp, the skier should pull out to the left side of the boat wake, setting up a little wider than the jump ramp, about 200 feet before the jump.

As you hit the ramp, it's very important to maintain your body position. This shouldn't be difficult, since you should have mastered this when you went over the corner. Your skis will be on the ramp about two beats longer than they were when you went off the corner, so you'll have to concentrate that much longer on maintaining the proper body position. Don't pull on the rope, make sure your weight is evenly distributed on both feet, and as you come up to the lip of the ramp look at the horizon at least 200 feet out from the ramp. Keep your eyes up throughout the jump. If you look down, you'll fall down. Remember, looking down causes your ski tips to go straight down.

LANDING

In jump competition, the jump doesn't count unless you ski away, so your landing is important. When you land in the water from the height of 25 to 30 feet up with a good lift and speed, as an advanced skier will, your skis will sink in the water a good bit, but it is still a glancing blow. In order to be able to ski away you must maintain good body position. Sometimes skiers fall over the back of their skis, sitting down on them. This is fine, and it's a natural reaction, but if you land this way you must be sure your hands are low because when you sit back it is difficult to get up again.

If you come off the ramp upside down, which could happen the first few times, it's probably because you didn't freeze in your body position and you pulled on the rope while on the ramp. Or

You can sit down after landing from a jump, but you must ski away for the jump to count in competition.

Some people land almost standing up, allowing their knees to absorb the shock.

you were in perfect position coming off the top but you looked down, so the tips of your skis pointed down. If you look to the side, the skis will go the opposite direction of the way you're looking.

I've heard people say falling off a jump ramp is akin to falling off a high dive, which isn't so bad. Everyone falls from time to time. But I've also seen people get the wind knocked out of them, even break their ribs. All the more reason to learn to maintain good body position.

If there were a scientific formula for long jumps it would read: speed + lift = distance. So once you are consistently successful at riding over the ramp, you can begin to increase your distance; you do this by adding a little spring to get lift off the jump ramp. Some people do this naturally. The lift or spring is begun as your knees bend when you come onto the ramp. As you cross the surface of the ramp your natural reaction is to resist or push against the hardness of the ramp; the more you can exaggerate this natural reflex of your knees, the better your lift will be. If you think of springing at the bottom of the ramp, by the time you react, your spring will happen at the lip, or top edge, of the jump ramp. Springing seems to be much easier for short-legged skiers—they can extend their legs more quickly than a long-legged person.

After you've learned the technique of springing, you need to work on combining it with "cutting," or generating speed *before* you get on the ramp. Maintaining the lift off the top of the ramp remains vital, as the formula above makes clear. In pro competition you often see a skier crush, or not get any lift at all. Usually this happens because the skier is out of body position.

ADVANCED TECHNIQUES

GOING THE DISTANCE— SINGLE WAKE CUT

In your first tries at jumping, you'll probably go about 30 feet. The pros call this relatively short jumping distance "plopping over" the ramp. And to them, it *is* just plopping over, since the men consistently jump in the 180-foot-plus range and the women in the high 130s and 140s. Once you've mastered "plopping over" with the boat speed at the maximum for your age, developed a little natural spring, and have gotten hooked on the excitement of jumping, you'll want to prolong that sensation by going longer distances. The first step to going farther is to generate speed or "cutting to the ramp." The basic technique is a single wake cut.

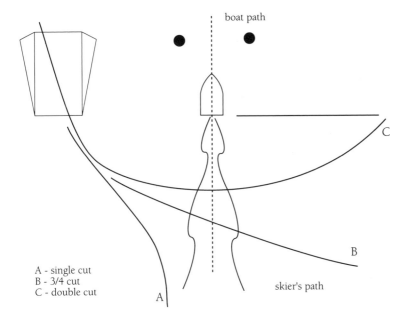

boat path

C

B

skier's path

A - single cut
B - 3/4 cut
C - double cut

A

This diagram shows the progressive approaches to the ramp, starting with a single cut.

The best way to learn is to have your driver, over a series of sets, gradually move away from the jump ramp until he gets to the point where he's driving in the boat path marked by the jump course buoys. There are two buoys that make up the boat path. The one nearest the ramp is 45 feet away, the farthest is 60 feet away. The boat path is a straight line between these buoys.

Since the distance between the boat and the jump ramp is wider than it was when you were "plopping over," you have to pull to the left from directly behind the boat at a different point in order to reach the ramp. This is "cutting" in to the ramp. In your early sessions, you pulled out about 200 feet before the ramp; for this technique, you wait until the boat is closer to the water line (the bottom) of the ramp. When the boat is about parallel to the ramp, you start your cut.

Your body position for this technique is basically the same as it is for beginning jumping technique; now you just add extra pressure to your right ski, letting your legs do the work, and not leaning over or away with the upper body. Keep the weight on the balls of your feet and keep both skis edging smoothly all the way to the bottom of the ramp, using the tug-of-war pulling technique of slalom skiing. I know it may sound strange to approach the ramp with your skis on their edges, but as the skis hit the ramp surface they flatten out automatically.

This photo shows the cut or speed phase of jumping; note the skis on an aggressive edge and the tug-of-war body position.

In the spring or lift phase, the legs are almost straight at the lip of the ramp.

The distance phase is where the jumper enjoys the fruits of his labor— free flight. It's the closest thing to flying there is.

The first few times you try this you'll probably be hitting the ramp somewhere in the center, skiing diagonally to the top left and out and away from the boat. Once you get the hang of cutting into the bottom, you'll find yourself edging harder and harder while maintaining proper body position. When you gain more speed and momentum, couple this with a spring, and you'll jump farther.

THREE-QUARTER CUT

The next phase of cutting is a three-quarter cut. Ski out over both wakes to the right side of the boat (if you look up at the boat, you will be about even with the transom) and then swing back to the left, cutting on the edge of your skis and pulling all the way into the bottom of the ramp. This is just an extension of cutting into the ramp, but because you are crossing both wakes, you are covering more distance and have more time to generate speed. Many pro skiers spend time practicing a three-quarter cut as it is easier to work on body position for the spring.

DOUBLE-CUT

Once you've mastered the three-quarter cut, confidently crossing the boat wakes and edging tug-of-war fashion onto the jump ramp while maintaining good lift, it's time to learn the technique pro skiers use—the double-cut. Pro skiers using this technique have been clocked at over 70 mph going into the bottom of the ramp. Obviously, such speeds come at a very high level of skiing proficiency, but by applying the technique, you'll increase your own proficiency and add to the fun of jumping.

The double-cut is exactly what it sounds like. The skier starts wide on the left side of the boat, then swings out to the right side of the boat and crosses both wakes in a crack-the-whip fashion to gain more speed. As he swings to the right of the boat, the skier actually passes the boat with his generated speed before making the turn to the ramp.

To visualize how this works, think about a pendulum. The boat is the fulcrum of the pendulum, and you, the skier, are the stone on the end of the pendulum. Wherever you leave from width-wise, you should land at that distance on the other side, after going over the ramp while springing and maintaining the proper cut to generate speed.

To achieve this, the skier does a series of cuts to get as wide as possible on the right side of the boat. When the driver lines up with the jump (about 1,500 to 1,800 feet away from the ramp), the skier will be in line with the center of the ramp. Two buoys are positioned 500 to 600 feet away from the lip of the ramp. The 500- and 600-foot buoys are part of the jump course and are used by the skier to mark the distance to the ramp. For a double-cut, a skier will pull out wide to the left, swing around or between the 500- and 600-foot buoys, and cut (the first cut) to the right, arcing wide up to the boat. Then, at the proper moment, he will cut to the left (the second) and go over the ramp.

For a triple cut the skier zigzags three times to gain speed and gain width on the boat. Generally you'll see a skier take a quick swing to the right at about 750 feet, then make a hard cut out to the left side of the boat. At this point, the skier will come up on the 500- and 600-foot buoys; they are there to help the skier's timing, but he's not required to go around them. The faster the boat's going, the more time the skier needs for his swing, so a male pro skier with boat speed of 35 mph may cut very close to the 600-foot buoy, around 625 or right on top of it. A skier going a little slower, such as a pro woman at 32 mph, may cut somewhere near 550 or so, in between the two buoys. The even slower speeds of junior skiers (30 mph and under) will allow skiers to cut later, often very close to the 500-foot buoy or just after it.

When the skier cuts to the left side, toward the 500- and 600-foot buoys, he gives a sharp, short pull that swings him up wide on the left side of the boat. Then, in order to slow down without getting slack in the rope, he quickly does a maneuver that resembles snow plowing on snow skis, pushing his legs very far apart and rolling on to the inside edges of the skis. At the moment he wants to turn, he pulls the skis back together, whips them around, and points them 90 degrees straight across the wakes to the right.

At this point the skier is really going to be edging hard with the left ski and maintaining that good, tug-of-war body position with hips up to handle, back straight, leveraging against the boat for all he's worth. A lot of pros, as they come off the second wake, will just land on the left ski with their right ski still in the air to reduce drag. The skier will stay in this pull and lean away from the boat, in good body position, until he's about even with the back corner of the boat. At that point he gives a sharp jerk with the line across his waist, still skiing on the left ski only.

The combination of these motions will actually throw the skier, moving faster than the boat, up past the boat. Depending upon where the skier cut—at the 500- or 600-foot buoy—he's got anywhere from 150 to 200 feet to glide up on the boat before he needs to make the turn to the jump ramp.

Once the skier is out in front of the boat, he'll pull his right ski down and glide along with the boat, with his left arm extended toward the jump ramp so the line is taut. His weight is centered on the skis on the balls of the feet, his knees are pushed well forward, and his shoulders face forward, not turned toward the ramp.

This is where the real courage is required in jumping. This is the point when the skier must decide how long he wants to wait before he cuts back across the wakes and onto the jump surface while still remaining in control. The reward for proper timing is lots of speed onto the ramp. The penalty for bad timing is an unplanned meeting with the side of the ramp and a nasty spill. Timing comes with lots of practice.

To time this crucial cut, most pro skiers will look down the extended line to the bow of the boat to sight where the boat is in relation to the jump. For example, if the bow has covered up most of the ramp a skier may think he is starting too late, feeling that if he turns and cuts for the ramp he will not make it onto the ramp surface and will hit the side curtain. If there's still a fair distance between the bow and the bottom corner of the ramp, he may feel he's started too early and will miss the whole ramp.

When to go is a matter of personal choice and judgment. Once the skier's made that decision, he'll turn toward the ramp, making a smooth turn with his skis together, the right ski just barely in front of the left, pushing progressively. He'll be in the same tug-of-war body position, leveraging away from the boat, hands low, skis on edge.

A lot of jumpers let the boat pull them up out of this position as they cross the wakes. When this happens you actually lose speed onto the bottom of the ramp, as well as getting thrown into an unstable position, losing the tug-of-war with the boat. This generally happens when the skier's turn is too fast and hard and the skier can't brace against the pull of the boat. The turn should be smooth and controlled with the line always taut. When you're aiming at the jump ramp at well over 60 mph, you definitely want to be stable.

Once the skier has come off the second wake, he'll continue to hold the edge all the way to the bottom of the ramp. If he hasn't waited too long to cut he'll come close to the bottom right corner of the ramp, ski diagonally across it, and go off the top left. By the time you can do this, springing has become a natural reaction and as soon as your legs hit the ramp you unleash them.

BALKING—THE SAFETY VALVE

If a skier mistakenly waits too long to cut to the jump ramp and he realizes in the middle of the wakes that he won't make it onto the surface, there's a safety procedure called "balking," or refusing the jump. A skier lets go of the handle and skis wide around the left side of the jump without going over it.

Knowing how to balk safely is imperative, and it's well worth practicing. If you lose control you're a lot better off balking than going into the jump without control and risking the possibility of crashing. It is possible to hit the corner of the ramp with the fins of the skis and make it over without crashing, but it's not something I'd count on.

One note about aiming for the ramp. Skiers tend to look at the bottom-right corner; however, you should apply one of the same principles you use in slalom. If you look at the buoy, you'll ski right into it. The same is true of the corner of the ramp. Narrow your focus and look at the top-left corner. This will keep you on track up the center of the ramp and will keep your head up, which helps maintain your body position and allows for spring.

As a child, I had a hard time convincing myself to wait long enough to gain lots of speed onto the jump. To help me overcome this, my father put out what he called a cut buoy for me. This buoy was placed in the area where the skier makes the final turn and cut to the ramp, which trained me to swing wider on the right side of the boat, as well as making me wait longer to

Learning to balk safely is a must.

turn for the ramp and gain speed. Once I got up the courage to go around this buoy and see that I could make it onto the ramp without hitting the side, my father and brother would sneak out each evening and move the buoy farther down the course a little, without my knowing it. So each day in practice I was getting later and later to the ramp without knowing it. This was a sneaky training technique, but I did set the Junior Girls jumping record twice that year, and continued to set records long after that.

QUICK TIPS

- Learn jumping from a qualified coach.
- Wear proper safety equipment.
- Practice body position on dry land.
- On the first try over the ramp, hold proper body position, or freeze.
- Start by going over the right corner of the jump, not the whole ramp.
- If you look down, you fall down.
- For advanced skiers, practice safe balking so if you lose control, you'll know how to avoid the ramp.
- To increase distance, work your way up through single wake cuts, three-quarter cuts, double wake cuts, and finally triple wake cuts with the help of a coach.

SEVEN

TRICK
SKIING

TRICK SKIING used to be called "hot dogging" in the old days and evokes memories of Ricky McCormick and Alan Kempton performing aerial maneuvers like snow-ski "hot doggers"— ramp flips and all sorts of one-of-a-kind tricks. Today, "hot dogging" describes the high-water jumps and barrel rolls often performed on local lakes and generally done on a slalom-type ski. "Free style" is the term for the amazing ramp tricks, double flips, and double turns done on jump skis at Cypress Gardens and in ski shows around the world. They are breathtaking—and sometimes so wild that you begin to question the sanity of the skiers.

The granddaddy of all these modern hybrids is competitive trick skiing. The sport has come a very long way since the days of Al Tyll on his "banana peels"—the nickname should give you a good idea of what it's like to ski on them. The changes in equipment alone are mind-boggling. The old "banana peels" were extra-long (50 inches or more), very narrow, and made of wood. Today's trick skis are much shorter than other types of skis, only 36 to 44 inches in length, wider at 8 to 10 inches, designed without fins on the bottom, and made from the same high-tech materials as slalom and jump skis.

Most high-performance trick skis are made by the compres-

My brother Sammy Duvall, four-time World Overall Champion, shows winning form on the front flip.

sion-molding process, as RIM skis cannot withstand the banging around a pro tricker puts his skis through. Tips come in different shapes—most trick skis have a somewhat squared tip, but you'll also see some with very round tips, as well as the elliptical, a hybrid of the two.

Trick skis come in pairs or as a single ski. Pairs may be of the RIM-type, because they are typically beginning trick skis and aren't subjected to the forces of pro skiers. Pro skiers and top-level trick ski competitors ski on a single trick ski that is lighter and substantially stiffer than a RIM pair of tricks. A single ski will be nearly as expensive, if not more, because of the labor-intensive compression molding.

The bindings on trick skis can be any of those we've discussed, from adjustable to double-high wrap plate. The difference between the bindings for trick skis and slalom skis is the placement of the rear binding. On a single trick ski, the back binding will be cocked at an angle, not set directly in line with the front binding as on a slalom ski. For example, if you're a right-foot-forward skier, the left foot will point to the left. This foot position enables you to drive the ski in different directions quickly and easily.

The angle at which your binding is on the ski is a matter of personal preference. If you think about the ski as a clock, with your front foot at twelve (assuming it's your right foot), then your left binding might be set at nine, ten, or even eleven. Only an open toe binding is used, because an advanced trick skier will take his rear foot in and out of the binding to perform different types of tricks.

An interesting point of the design of trick skis is that the bottom platform is a little bit wider than the top. The side cuts or edges of a trick ski actually angle up and in toward the surface the skier stands on. This side cut is almost an inch wide and is usually covered with rubber for safety. Because the bottom of the ski is wider than the top, when the ski spins around on the water it won't catch an edge. The edges, in fact, are almost like a knife, allowing the trick ski to be able to edge without a fin. Trick skis do have rocker (the bend from tip to tail), like a slalom ski.

The ropes for trick skiing are also specialized. The length is about half as long as a slalom line and the handle is a little longer than a standard slalom or jump handle. Inside the rope vee of the handle is a canvas sling called a "bear trap" or "toe strap"; this allows skiers to secure the rope to their foot for the series of tricks called toe tricks. If you intend to learn any toe tricks, you should invest in a quick release, which is a contraption that allows the rope to be disengaged from the pylon instantly. It works this way: the rope is looped through a hook mechanism on the release that allows the observer in the boat to "release" the rope from the boat if the skier falls suddenly while performing tricks with the toe strap on. This safety device was invented to help avoid knee injuries caused by the quick falls taken while doing toe turns.

TRICK SKIING

Trick skiing is generally done at a slow speed, making it particularly popular with children. In competition, the skier may pick any speed he wishes, depending on his skill level, height, and weight. For example, a small child might want to go 12 mph, while many-time world-record holder Cory Pickos runs the boat at 20 mph.

Trick skiing has a large following because you don't need much equipment other than your skis, a proper rope, and a boat. It's not even necessary to have a powerful boat, since trick skiing is done at such slow speeds. It's also a fun way to challenge your skiing skills if you don't have access to a slalom course or jump ramp, as the amateur competitive set has discovered. In recent years, trick skiing has had a resurgence of popularity on the Professional Association of Water Skiers (PAWS) pro tour because format changes and spectacular tricks have been added to the pro rule book.

BASIC TECHNIQUES

It's best to start out "tricking" on two skis, mastering the basic skills, before moving on to one ski. Trick skiing is definitely a discipline, similar to gymnastics or ballet, in which your skills build upon each other. Therefore, it's very important to get your basics down to an automatic reaction before attempting more challenging tricks.

There are definitely some differences in getting up on trick skis compared to other skis. First, let's go back to why the skis were called "banana peels." They feel very slippery because they have no fins to stabilize their lateral movement. When you're getting up it's important to keep your knees bent so the skis don't slide every which way.

Often, when teaching students to trick ski, I tell them to stay in a sitting position, even after the skis are on a plane, so they can get used to the way the skis feel on a plane before using just their legs to get into skiing position.

Once you're up it's like learning to ski on two skis all over again. You should try edging back and forth across the wake, to get a feel for the way the skis move in the water and the speed you need to be going. It's similar to learning ice skating or roller skating for the first time, and you'll feel entirely out of control at first. You'll need to shift your weight onto the ski opposite the direction you want to go, gently and gradually, without making any sudden moves.

Speed for trick skiing is a matter of personal preference. You shouldn't be going so slowly that your skis are sinking and it's work to stay up on the water. Nor should you be going so fast that you don't have control of the skis and they wobble and shake. Try to find a speed somewhere in between these two. Use hand signals to communicate with your driver, giving an "okay" sign (index finger and thumb in closed circle) when the speed is just right.

The proper body position
for trick skiing is similar
to that for combo skiing.

Once you've learned how the skis work and have established a comfortable speed, it's time to start building your skills by learning some basic tricks.

There's an endless array of tricks to be learned, from the basic two-ski side slide to a flip with twists like the professionals do on the tour. This is one of the appealing things about trick skiing —there's always something new to be learned.

There are several categories of tricks. Most tricks can be done on one or two skis and in a basic or reversed direction. The various categories include surface turns, which means that the ski never leaves the surface of the water; wake turns, which means the same tricks performed in the air when crossing over

TRICK SKIING

145

the wake; and step-over tricks, where the skier steps over the rope while turning. These tricks can be performed on either one or two skis, over the wake or on the surface.

Then there are toe tricks, done only on one ski, either on the surface or over the wake, with one foot in the "toe strap." And then there are the pro-level tricks, which are a whole different world. Toe steps combine wake tricks with one foot in the toe strap and the other foot (with the ski on) stepping over the line. Flips are exactly what they sound like—forward or backward somersaults over the wake. And body-overs, or ski-line tricks, are where a skier actually jumps over the towline. The toe steps, flips, and body-overs are the types of tricks you'll see on the pro tour, and are incredible to watch!

GET BACK TO BASICS

THE 180

The easiest trick to learn is the basic 180-degree turn, which is simply going from a forward skiing position to a backward skiing position. Each trick is a building block for future tricks you'll learn, and the 180 is your foundation.

As with every new skill in water skiing, the first thing to learn is good body position. For trick skiing your knees should be bent, feet shoulder-width apart, back straight and strong, and eyes on the horizon. Your arms should be slightly bent.

When learning the 180, most people literally don't know which way to turn. Usually you will feel more comfortable turning one way than another. People who ski with their left foot forward on a slalom ski usually turn better to the left, and right-foot-forward skiers turn better toward the right. That's not always true, though, so do what feels most natural to you.

If you are skiing in good body position and feel ready to turn, gently pull the rope in to your waistline. This has the effect of advancing you toward the boat. The boat's pulling you all the time, so if you don't advance yourself, the boat will pull the rope out of your hand when you attempt the turn. Once you've advanced on the boat, if you're turning to the right, let go with your right hand. Think about driving your skis around a pivot point, and lead with your head and shoulders to initiate the turn. Don't

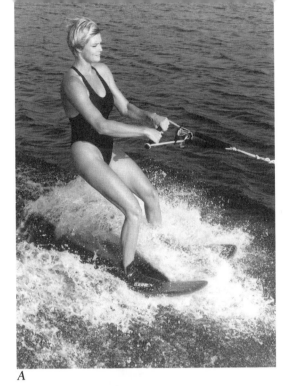

A

initiate the turn by leaning away from the boat. And keep your body weight directly over the center of the skis.

When I learned to trick ski as a child, my father used an example you may find helpful. He would hold a pencil vertically and twist it. If the pencil was leaned off its pivot point, it would fall, but if you kept it straight up and down, it would turn. Try to visualize your body as the pencil—you must stay upright on the pivot point over the skis to avoid falling.

On your way to the back position, reach around for the handle with your right hand. As you spin to the back, your arm will naturally turn over from a palm down to a palm up position, so as long as the rope is close to your body you should be able to grab it easily, palm skyward, at your back.

If you have the correct body position, you should be able to ski backwards standing with your knees bent, weight on the balls of your feet, back fairly straight, and your eyes on the horizon. Stay in that position a while, until you feel stable.

When you're ready to turn back to the front, let go of the

handle with your right hand again and maintain your good body position. The pull of the boat will swing you back in the direction you came from. Coming to the front is really easy.

At this point some coaches recommend learning how to edge the skis back and forth, just as you did when you were skiing forward. This is a great idea, especially because it's a good practice technique for future tricks.

COMMON ERRORS

Two things often go wrong when you're learning this trick. First, it is possible to have the handle high up in the center of your back. If you do this, the rope is then too high for your center of gravity. The pull of the boat will topple you onto your back.

You may also bend at the waist too much and find yourself looking down into the water. If this happens, you will fall away from the boat, face first, into the water. I often recommend an exaggerated stance for beginners, telling my students to think of putting the handle right underneath their behind as they get into the back position, almost as if they were going to sit on it.

SIDE SLIDE

One trick that looks good to recreational skiers, although it's not high in point value for competition, is called a side slide. It's exactly what it sounds like. Your skis are turned in either direction, 90 degrees to the boat, and they slide along sideways.

One of the reasons most coaches will teach you to do a 180 before the side slide is that it's actually a little easier to do a complete turn as opposed to stopping the skis halfway. Also, during the side slide the skis bump along sideways in the turbulence behind the boat and can be a little difficult to keep in position.

One of the biggest mistakes beginners make with the side slide is thinking the edges will catch and pull them into the water, so they lean away from the boat. If you lean away from the boat you will invariably raise your hands too high and then fall to the side, away from the boat.

A good body position: weight is well balanced over the skis, the handle is low, and the knees are well bent to absorb the turbulence of the prop wash.

To do a side slide successfully, your hands should be at waist level and pulled in close to your side. The motion for starting a side slide is the same technique we discussed for the 180—giving a tug on the rope to advance on the boat.

Having an edge catch is one of the trick skier's most dreaded falls. Most of the falls in trick skiing aren't very bad, but when an edge catches, it slaps you down so fast you don't know what happened. I've had the breath knocked out of me when I've caught an edge. It can happen on any trick. Usually, the cause of the fall is that your knees aren't bent enough, or your body position is wrong, or your timing was off over the wake. This is one of the main reasons it's important to have a quick release operator who's alert and aware of the tricks you're doing, especially on toe (when your foot is strapped to the rope) and line tricks, where there's a chance of the free leg tangling in the rope. Your release person must have quick hands and pay close attention at all times.

THE 360

To spin all the way around and do a 360 turn, you link two 180s together. The difference is that when you get to the back, instead of letting go with the same hand (in our example, the right hand), you'll let go with the opposite hand (in our example, the left), so that you do a full, front-to-front turn. Start slowly with a 180 to the back and a 180 continuing in the same direction, then decrease the pause in the back position between turns until you do the whole turn in one, smooth motion. Eventually, with enough practice, there will be no hitch in the back at all and you'll sail smoothly all the way around.

A good body position is the start of every trick. From here the rope is tugged into the waist.

The rope is on its way into the waist; the knees are bent but pushing the skis into the turn. Eyes and head are starting the turn, body weight is on the pivot point.

Weight is shifted onto the balls of the feet; the handle is close to the body so that the right hand can grasp the handle smoothly.

In the beginning stages of learning a 360-degree turn, the back position is where a skier should stop or hesitate so as to maintain control and body position.

The left hand has released the handle and the spin continues to the right. Note the weight is centered over the skis and the body is upright.

CAMILLE DUVALL

Once you've mastered both the 180 and the 360 behind the boat, you should practice them over the wakes to build your skills further.

WAKE 360

In order to receive credit from the five judges in tournaments, wake tricks must be done "in the air." In other words, they are done *over* the wake, not on it.

In general, it's easier to learn wake tricks from the outside of the wakes coming in, because the crest or lip of the wake tosses a skier into the air with proper timing. However, as your skills become more advanced, you should learn the trick going out of the wakes as well, because it makes it easier to design a "trick run." In competition, a skier is allowed to put together as many different tricks as possible in two nonstop sequences each lasting 20 seconds. The more tricks you can do, the higher the score.

The continuation of the spin almost to the start position; the weight is still in the center of the skis and the handle is still close to the waist.

Back to where you started from.

To start a wrap, snap the handle into the body; the final position of the handle will be even with the right hip.

Pull the rope hard past the right hip.

Pull the handle a little past the body so you can reach it easily behind the back.

In a split second, grasp the handle with the left hand and reach forward with the right to the rope bridle.

The hand holding the fat braided part of the rope supports the skier with the pull of the boat.

A fairly impressive trick that's easy to learn is the 360 spin over the wake on two skis. This can be done using a hand-to-hand method or with a method called the wrap.

Wrapping is a technique that's good to learn because it will come into play when you advance to 540-degree spins (circle and a half) and 720-degree spins (two circles). It's like making yourself into an old-fashioned spinning top.

Let's assume you turn to the left very easily. To learn to wrap, go outside the right wake of the boat, so you will be performing

TRICK SKIING

155

After you are wrapped and outside the wake, start a strong controlled edge with weight on the balls of the feet from about 5 feet off the crest of the wake with all of the pull of the boat on the right hand.

At the crest of the wake, pull with the right hand sharply on the rope and give a little hop. Start the turn with your head.

Let the pull of the rope unwind you, keeping your weight centered over the skis and the handle close to your body.

the trick from outside the wake and landing in the center. Take the handle in a baseball-style grip and pull it in toward you very hard and quick, snapping it to your right hip. Quickly reach behind your back with your left hand, grab the handle, remove your right hand from the handle, and grab the rope up the bridle about 18 inches in front of you. With this quick movement you will have advanced way up on the boat and the handle will come up easily on your back. (Note: A lot of the trick harnesses have a fat, braided portion that is easy to get a grip on.) Ski straight and get your balance.

You're still skiing forward at this point. Begin edging your skis toward the wake (you should be no more than five feet from it). As the skis come to the crest of the wake (the sharp part on the edge), let your tips pass through it; as your bindings hit the crest, give a sharp tug with your right hand on the line. Turn your head and shoulders to the left so you are unwinding out of the rope. Once you initiate this turn, let go with your right hand and the boat will unwind you in midair. You may find it necessary to give a little hop at the crest of the wake so you do the entire trick in the air. The key is to maintain your body axis straight up and down all the way through the turn and keep the handle close to your body. It's easy to let the rope unravel, which will automatically make you spin. Keep in mind the wrap can be done on either side of the body for doing spins in either direction.

Look around toward the boat, keeping the handle in close.

Reach for the handle and you'll feel yourself completing the turn and landing.

COMMON ERRORS

Once people learn this trick they feel the need to swing way out to the side of the boat, thinking the farther from the wakes the more speed they will generate. Most people think speed gives them more air on the trick, and it can, but if you're planning to learn other tricks and put them together in a cohesive trick run, this is a bad habit to develop. Too much speed will throw you all the way off the far wake. To generate speed correctly, start about five feet from the wake, make a strong controlled edge into the wake, and use your hand on the rope to pull you into the spin. A controlled edge will have the same effect of throwing you higher, but you'll land with better body position in the center of the two wakes and be in a good position to do another trick. Remember, in a trick run you only have twenty seconds, so you don't want to waste valuable time skiing into position. You save time if you land in position.

STEP-OVERS

Another easy trick to learn on two skis is a step-over from back to front. This consists of one ski actually stepping over the rope. While a step-over can be done from skiing forward to backward or skiing backward to forward, it's usually easiest to learn it stepping from the back to front first.

To set up, do your regular 180 from front to skiing backward. Once you are turned toward the back, maneuver the rope so that it's pushed down low.

Take one hand off of the rope and reach between your legs and grab the handle. Once you are secure, take the other hand and put it between your legs on the handle so that both of your hands are between your legs. Once you are stable skiing in this position, making sure your head and eyes are up and your knees well bent, keep your back straight, shift your weight onto the right ski, and lift your left ski with the rear tip touching your behind. (For all our examples, we'll assume you're a right-foot-forward skier. A left-foot-forward skier would use opposite feet and hand positions.) Initiate the turn with your head and shoulders and the boat will spin you back around to the front. As long as your ski is raised you will automatically step over the rope. It's

Start at the back in good skiing position.

Break at the waist a little to get the handle just above your knees. Be sure to keep your eyes up during this process.

Reach between the legs with one hand.

And then with the other hand—so both hands are between the legs.

Before attempting to lift the ski over the rope, you must get your back upright.

Shift your weight onto the right ski and lift the left ski and look toward the boat.

CAMILLE DUVALL

160

Be sure the back tip of the ski is close to or touching your behind so the ski will be sure to clear the rope. Keep the back very straight but the knees bent.

The body stays upright as the ski clears the line—the handle is held close to the body.

As the ski touches the water, think of shifting your weight onto the balls of your feet and reach for the handle with your free hand.

really important that when you lift the ski up you tap yourself in the buns with it to be sure it goes over the line. If the ski goes under the towline you'll fall. If you have trouble lifting the ski, you may want to try to let go with one hand and hold it out for balance. (Use your left hand for balance if you're turning toward the left, and vice versa.) This helps keep your back straight and it is easier to lift the ski from this position.

Stepping over to the back is basically the same process, but it's a little harder because you have to initiate the advancing on the boat, then step over with one ski. A common mistake is leaning the head and shoulders away from the boat (remember the pencil?) instead of turning and forgetting about using the bottom half of the body, so the skier falls away from the boat without getting the ski over the line.

To initiate the step-over to the back, concentrate on that sharp pull into your waist or lower to advance on the boat, shift your weight onto the right ski, lift the left ski up with a bent knee while simultaneously turning the head and shoulders. As you turn your head and shoulders, your body will spin and the lifted ski will follow. At this point, the right hand should come off of the handle. Think of putting your knee over the line and the ski will follow. Remember to stay over your pivot point, not leaning away from the boat. It's a must to keep your knees well bent.

Some people feel this particular trick is actually easier to learn on one ski than on two because you don't have to put the ski over the line. However, the disadvantage to learning on one is that once your foot is over the line you have nothing to stand on, so I recommend learning it first on two skis.

Keep in mind that each of the two-ski tricks I've discussed are the foundation you're laying for learning all the rest of the tricks. Even pro tour skiers had to learn two-ski back-and-front tricks before they could advance to more difficult one-ski tricks. So I feel it's really important to learn the basics on two skis first, with perfect form. You will build better body position, understanding of rope handling, and spinning techniques. There is also more leeway for mistakes, which makes learning a little less frustrating.

I keep emphasizing the importance of learning on two skis because I so often had students who had never learned any basics on two skis but had wasted a lot of money on buying the fanciest, most expensive single trick ski they could find. To top it off, they

could only do one trick on one ski! These folks spent frustrating months trying to learn tricks on one ski because they had no foundation of basic trick skiing on two skis.

TOE HOLDS

This is one of the most impressive categories of tricks. Toe holds are almost a form of ballet at the professional level, and I have the utmost respect for skiers who are skilled at these tricks —which, by the way, are always done on one ski. These advanced tricks should be learned after mastering the one-ski 180, 360, wake back (WB), and wake front (WF).

The basic toe hold trick to learn is the toe hold 180 front to back. It's the easiest foundation for the rest of the series of toe tricks. Before you try any toe holds you need two things: a quick release on your pylon (and an observer to operate it) and a trick handle with a canvas toe strap.

The toe straps are designed so that when pressure is released from the handle (i.e., letting go with your hands), it will close and tighten around your foot.

Trick skiers have different theories about where the strap should actually fit on your foot. The term *toe strap* is actually a little misleading because it really goes around your entire foot. Most pro skiers and advanced trick competitors will use a 3-inch-wide strap and will have it way up almost around the arch of the foot for toe holds. Pros also use a heel strap that fits over the heel so during all of the twisting and jumping it is impossible for the strap to slide off. A lot of beginning skiers are afraid to commit themselves to having the rope that far up on the foot, so to combat their fears they put it on just the tips of their toes with no heel strap; when they attempt turns, it just slips off. The toe strap should be around the ball of the foot and should stay on when your toes are pointed up and the foot is flexed, but slide off easily when your toes are pointed toward the boat. You need to have great faith in the person holding the quick release for you, and they need to pay very close attention. Once you've got the strap on your foot where it feels comfortable, straighten your back, concentrate on good body position with your knee well bent, and keep your weight on the ball of your foot over the middle of the ski so that it will pivot easily.

Starting with a good body position, take your foot out of the rear binding and lift it into the toe strap; use a double overhand grip to keep the strap open.

Keeping the knee bent, wiggle the toes up into the strap until it feels comfortable but will stay on your foot as you let go of the handle.

Once the strap is on, let go with both hands and straighten your back. Keep the knee well bent to keep the ski under control. You can put your arms out to the side for balance.

To learn a toe back 180, as you ski along on one ski, take your back foot out of the binding—keep your knee well bent. While holding the handle with a double overhand grip (to keep the toe strap open), raise your leg and put your foot in the handle's toe strap.

Once you're comfortable you may hold your arms out to the sides for balance as if you were a tightrope walker. While it's a natural reaction, you should not flap your arms like a bird. Too much arm movement will rock you off your pivot point and make you fall. Learn to steer the ski back and forth between the wakes in this position.

When you're comfortable and well balanced you are ready to try turning to the 180 position. Go back and rely on the techniques you've learned from the very beginning for a 180 turn front to back. This time, of course, you'll be pulling the rope with your leg to advance yourself on the boat, which requires a smooth, strong, steady pull. Try not to pull your rope foot past the ski or kick yourself in the leg. Practice doing smooth pulls until it feels comfortable. Now you are ready; give a pull and as you feel yourself advancing, use your head and shoulders to initiate the turn and the ski will follow.

Once you reach the back position, think about keeping your eyes up and your shoulders level. Don't let one shoulder get lower than the other. Keep your arms out for balance and get a feel for the way the ski tracks going backwards over the water. Keep your weight on the ball of your foot and your rope leg pulled in.

When you're comfortable skiing backwards in this position, and feel you have your balance, you can turn back to the front.

Since you don't have a handle to let go of from the back, give a pull on the rope with your rope leg and turn your head and shoulders back toward the boat. As you spin to the front reach forward slightly and push your weight onto the ball of your skiing foot. As you reach the front position, shift your weight onto the ball of your foot to stabilize the ski.

The most common error people make while attempting this trick is to look down at the water instead of keeping their eyes on the horizon. Keeping your weight well over the pivot point of your ski, with your back straight and eyes up, is the key to doing this trick successfully.

Which direction you turn is very important; as mentioned

A

B

C

D

earlier, all the tricks in this book can be done in reverse, but when you reverse a toe hold you will turn into your other leg, and it's a much more difficult trick, one that is best learned from a top-flight trick coach. As an example, if your ski is on your right foot, you'll turn toward the right, so that your legs will be in what I can only describe as an "open" position. If you turn left, in toward your other leg, you'll be doing a very advanced trick called a reverse toe back (RTB).

Remember, dry land practice is a big plus in learning the motions of any trick.

COMPETITION

The format for trick skiing competition is two 20-second passes in front of five judges who are seated along the shore line with a good view of the trick course. A skier attempts to do as many different tricks as possible without falling in the total 40 seconds and the skier with the highest point total is declared the winner.

THE TRICK COURSE

Official Trick Course

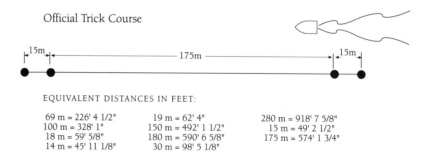

EQUIVALENT DISTANCES IN FEET:

69 m = 226' 4 1/2"	19 m = 62' 4"	280 m = 918' 7 5/8"
100 m = 328' 1"	150 m = 492' 1 1/2"	15 m = 49' 2 1/2"
18 m = 59' 5/8"	180 m = 590' 6 5/8"	175 m = 574' 1 3/4"
14 m = 45' 11 1/8"	30 m = 98' 5 1/8"	

As you can see from the diagram, there are two buoys, 650 feet apart, on each end of the trick course. These buoys are placed one after the other, not side by side like a set of boat gates in the slalom course. A skier may start his run whenever he is ready at any place between the two buoys. Because 20-second trick runs are timed from the shore, the timer starts the stopwatch as the skier begins performing his first trick. If he hasn't started by the time he passes the second buoy, the timer on shore starts the stopwatch automatically. So it's to the skier's advantage to start his run by the time he reaches that second buoy. Otherwise, he stands to lose precious time.

Once you start your run, you can do as many different tricks in the AWSA rule book as you possibly can in 20 seconds without falling. You cannot repeat a trick. At the end of 20 seconds you'll hear an air horn or buzzer; this tells you that your time is up.

Before you take to the water you must turn in a list of the tricks you plan to do in the order in which you plan to do them. Skiers call this their "dream sheet," indicating how rarely they actually succeed in completing every trick on the list.

The five judges determine if you get "credit" for all of the tricks you perform. There are certain criteria they'll be looking for (indicated in the rule book). Just as in a diving or gymnastics competition, each trick is assigned a specific point value. The judges award points or not based on the requirements that should be fulfilled for each trick. You either receive credit or full points for the trick or you receive none. To receive credit and accumulate points, you must receive credit for each trick from three of the five judges.

The second pass immediately follows the first. The boat turns around after the first run and returns through the course in the opposite direction. You then have another 20 seconds to perform different tricks; you are not allowed to repeat any of the tricks performed in the first pass. If you fall on a trick you do not receive credit for that trick and that particular run is ended. Therefore, staying on your skis is important. To give you an idea, depending upon the difficulty of their tricks, the top male pro skiers can do anywhere from 15 to 17 advanced tricks in 20 seconds, which is truly amazing. These pros are able to perform this many tricks because they maintain proper body position throughout the trick, so they are immediately ready for the next trick. When I was in tricking competition about the most I could ever get would be 12 or 13 tricks and I was only ranked third in the world at my peak.

There are an infinite number of tricks to learn, and putting together a run for competition that you can perform consistently and in 20 seconds is never easy. It is important that a skier learn tricks that fit and flow together easily so that no time is lost moving from trick to trick.

Many a trick skier has a love-hate relationship with his stopwatch. There's something about "having" to do your run in 20 seconds. Many top skiers, in an effort to feel the tournament time pressure, have the observer time their runs with a stopwatch. The observer starts the watch with the skier's first trick and at the end of 20 seconds can blow a whistle, honk the boat horn, or even yell "beep" to let the skier know 20 seconds are up. It's a great idea even for a novice to practice this way. Try timing your runs a few times before the first competition so you have a feel for it before competing.

PASS 1

Trick	Points	Description
SS	20	side slide
RSS	20	reverse side slide
B	30	180 turn, front to back
F	30	180 turn, back to front
RB	30	reverse 180 turn, front to back
RF	30	reverse 180 turn, back to front
O	40	360 turn, front to front
RO	40	reverse 360 turn, front to front
WB	50	wake 180 turn, front to back
WF	50	wake 180 turn, back to front
RWB	50	wake 180 turn, back to front off opposite wake
RWF	60	wake 180 turn, front to back also off the same wake

PASS 2

Trick	Points	Description
BOOC	0	180 turn, front to back done outside of course (OOC) (this takes time to set up with rope between the legs and therefore is done before the 20 seconds start)
LF	70	180 turn, back to front stepping over the line
WO	110	360 turn, over the wake done from the wrapped position (ski outside the wake and set up)

Then repeat any tricks from the first pass that were not performed within the 20-second time limit.

A common error that is seen all too often in tricks is a skier rushing through his runs, causing him to falter. There are two problems with rushing: first, rushing makes body position go by the wayside and a fall soon follows, ending the run. Second, a skier performs the tricks sloppily and does not receive credit or points for the tricks he performs. And there's the rub: tricks must be done quickly to get as many done in 20 seconds as possible but slowly enough to maintain control and receive credit for the trick.

For example, see the very basic trick run on the opposite page. (The letter abbreviations are standard from the AWSA rule book.) This is a very basic run worth 630 total points. It's a good run for a beginner and leaves room for improvement. This simple trick run can make you see how hard doing a 10,000-point trick run really is.

As a skier becomes proficient at two-ski tricks and moves up to one-ski tricks, he might work toward upgrading his run:

FIRST PASS		SECOND PASS	
		(Start by wrapping before you enter the course.)	
Trick	*Points*	*Trick*	*Points*
2 skis		2 skis	
WO	110	BOOC	0
WB	50	LF	110
WF	50	1 ski	
RWB	50	SS	40
RWF	50	RSS	40
O	40	B	60
RO	40	F	60
B	30	RB	60
F	30	RF	60
RB	30	O	90
RF	30	RO	90
SS	20	WB	80
RSS	20	WF	80
TOTAL POINTS:	550	RWB	80
		RWF	80
		TOTAL POINTS:	930

The overall total for these two passes is 1,480 points.

The first pass stacks the tricks from the most difficult to the easiest. The theory behind stacking tricks in this manner is if you are running out of time, your lower-point tricks are the ones that will be done after time is up for no score. The second pass is stacked with easier one-ski tricks first. These are a little more difficult and stacking tricks this way allows you to build up to the hardest tricks in your run. Both of these runs are hypothetical, and not required for competition. These are basic blueprints for runs and could be arranged in any order to best suit skiers' strengths and weaknesses.

As time goes by and skiers learn more difficult tricks, they may drop the lower-point value tricks and add the more advanced tricks, building on everything they have learned. But beware of planning a difficult, high-point trick as your first trick—it could come back to haunt you.

The first Masters tournament I skied in was in 1975. The Masters ski tournament is comparable to the Masters golf tournament in pressure and prestige. I had skied very well in slalom and jump, finishing only ½ buoy and a few feet behind Liz Allen, the perennial Masters Overall champion. (She won this prestigious tournament nine times before she retired.) Liz was my role model and my coach when I was growing up and I have much respect for this gracious champion. The tournament finally came down to the tricks event. Liz took her turn at tricks and didn't happen to ski up to her normally great potential. With a good trick run I could pull ahead of her in the Overall battle. What a realization for a fourteen-year-old—a shot at beating the best in the world!

I did a great first pass and knew I needed to get every trick in the 20 seconds of my second pass, and do them cleanly to pull ahead of Liz Allen. I came in wrapped for a toe wake 360, rushed the turn, caught an edge, and was slapped against the water for a fall. And with that fall my chance of winning the Masters Overall title was slapped away. This is a good example of why you should not try to do your most difficult tricks first. When the pressure's on, it's best to start with the tricks you know you can perform every time.

QUICK TIPS

- Trick skiing is great for children because it's done at slow speeds and needs no special equipment other than trick skis.
- Trick skiing is learned step by step, building on basic skills and body position.
- Tricks should be learned first on two skis.
- Most tricks can be performed in both directions.
- The easiest trick to learn is a 180-degree turn. Build on the skills mastered in the 180 to learn the side slide. Then progress to a 360-degree turn by linking two 180-degree turns together.
- When learning new tricks, don't forgo the dry-land practice before you start.
- To get ready for competition, design a trick run with your easiest tricks first for your initial competition.
- Tricks in competition are judged by a point system, comparable to gymnastics or diving.
- Be prepared to start your trick run between the trick buoys to save valuable time.
- Maintain good body position so you're set up for the start of the next trick.
- If you stumble on a trick, don't flail into the next trick. Stop to regain your composure and body position. It may cost you a few seconds of time, but if you fall your run ends.
- Practice performing each trick smoothly and in control so you'll be in position to go immediately into the next trick.
- To warm up for competition, fix your rope to a tree or dock post and physically go through the motions while visualizing yourself on the water. This also improves rope handling as well as muscle memory.

E I G H T

KNEEBOARDING, BAREFOOTING, AND OTHER WAYS TO HAVE FUN

I LOVE THE CHALLENGE and thrill of slalom skiing and jumping and I'm sure you will, too. But there are lots of other ways to get out on the water and have a great time; so let's explore some of the water-skiing variations that offer different challenges and different sensations. Then, you can pick your "sport" according to your mood or your companions, or just on a whim.

KNEEBOARDING—THE QUIET REVOLUTION

Ten years ago you might have seen a random kneeboarder on a weekend. Now they're everywhere. This kneeling version of water skiing (known to many as "knee skiing") has exploded. The reasons are clear: it is the easiest form of water skiing, it doesn't require the strength or skill of actual water skiing, it's done at slow speeds, crashes are mild, and it can be done with an underpowered boat. And best of all, kids love it!

Let's start with equipment. There are two basic designs for kneeboards. The flat-bottom "slalom" kneeboards have less drag,

which makes it easy to switch from rail to rail (the side edges) across the wakes and when turning.

Convex bottom, "trick" kneeboards have lots of rocker (bend), which gives them lift off the wake. They are softer than the stiff slalom kneeboards, so when you hit a wake, they flex and give you lift. The convex bottom prevents you from catching the rails, just the opposite of the slalom boards.

Most kneeboards have grooves or channels on the sides for better tracking. Some come with fins, others without, and some have retractable fins. Fins are good for slalom use, but they won't allow the board to spin for tricks. Most beginners find it easier to learn on a board with fins. Boards with retractable fins, such as the O'Brien Black Magic kneeboard, make a good compromise for a first-time family purchase. The majority of boards are polyurethane shell and foam filled, although some expensive, custom boards have a foam core like surfboards and sailboards, and the newest variation is a compression-molded board made like a slalom ski.

Be sure to consider the foam pads on which your knees will rest when you're buying a board. The basic, low-end pads are just flat, and frankly, they can be rather uncomfortable. Higher-end kneeboards and trick kneeboard pads have "walls" of foam around the edge of the pad and hollows to keep your knees from moving around. Some pads offer extra protection and comfort with a center strip of foam that goes between your legs to prevent them from banging together. A new addition that makes kneeboarding more comfortable and helps control are ankle roll pads that support the bend in your foot while kneeling.

The strap, which is a seat-belt-like contraption, is an important consideration for first-time kneeboarders. Beginners need a strap that will release easily when they wipe out. A 2-inch width with a strip of Velcro is the best choice.

Pros and trick kneeskiers use a 3-inch-wide strap, which provides more control, leverage, and support when they want to pull up the nose to do tricks that involve "getting air." These straps may have an extra neoprene pad to go across the thighs and a double-Velcro closure to keep the strap from releasing during heavy-leverage tricks.

If you're a family looking for a good time, you'll want to buy a medium-priced board that will last a while and survive your kids' learning to flip and turn. As you (or they) move up in skill level, you may want to invest in a state-of-the-art trick board, designed for the serious kneeboarder.

Once you've purchased a board, there are a few basics to keep in mind. The average speeds for kneeboarding are slower than for traditional skiing. A person weighing around 165 pounds, for instance, will kneeboard at 20 mph. Heavier kneeboarders, up around 200 pounds, need to go only a little faster, say 22 mph. Skiers around 145 pounds need only 18 to 19 mph to get on a plane, and kids can go even slower than that. But personal preference for speed is fine.

Of course, you need a ski rope, and just about any type will do. Most experienced kneeboarders find that a slalom rope, with its convenient shortening loops, is ideal. Twenty-eight feet off the standard 75-foot slalom line, which is the third loop (usually yellow), is a good length for kneeboarding behind an inboard. If you'll be kneeboarding behind an outboard and you have a bridle on your transom, try 32 off (green, or fourth loop), which will give you a little shorter line to make up for where the rope attaches to the boat.

BEACH STARTS

As with all phases of skiing, there is an easy way and a difficult way to learn. The easiest way to learn to kneeboard is to do a beach start the first time out. Wrestling a kneeboard in deep

Lean back on the board with the back straight. Keep the weight on the back of the board so that the nose doesn't dip under as the boat pulls you off the shore.

water for the first time can be exhausting. You need a good, wide, sandy beach area, clear of debris. Your board should be about five or six feet from the water.

Kneel on the kneeboard and strap yourself in. Use the same rope handling techniques as a slalom beach start. Let the boat pull you off the shore. Remember to lean back against the pull of the boat and *keep your arms pulled in, not extended out.* You'll know immediately if you're doing this correctly, because if you're not, you'll do a face plant over the front of the board into the sand. Timing is not as critical as on slalom skis, because there is no weight shifting to be done, but the driver should concentrate on giving you a smooth, steady pull, not jerking you off the sand in a sudden motion.

DEEP-WATER STARTS

When you fall—and everyone does—and you're out in the middle of the lake, you'll need to know how to do a deep-water start. The preflight wait is the hard part. First, prepare your board by loosely threading the strap through the loop and closing it. A good measure of the right distance is to adjust the strap so that when it's closed it falls at about the edge of where the neoprene pad meets the polyurethane. In other words, it's loose enough for you to slip your knees under it but not so loose that it will just flop around when you do so.

Lie on the kneepad on your belly and grab the strap and rope handle (overhand) with both hands. You might find it easiest to just grab the strap with your thumbs as you hold on to the handle. This precaution keeps the water from pushing the strap out of position for your knees. If you keep it in position the strap will be ready for you to slip your knees in when you get up on the board.

Keep your feet behind you, rest your elbows on the board, and tell your driver to "hit it!" Again, it's very important for the driver to give you a steady, smooth pull rather than to punch it. When you get up on a plane, use your stomach muscles to pull both of your knees up under you at the same time. *Keep your upper body bent fairly low* while you do this, otherwise you may fall to one side. When your knees are tucked up under you, inch them to the edge of the neoprene pad, pull the strap over your knees, and tighten it.

To determine whether you're being pulled at the right speed and your rope is the proper length, get your board directly behind the boat and look at the wakes on either side of you. You should be three to four feet behind the rooster tail of the boat (that bump of water in the middle of the wake), and in horizontal alignment to the steepest part of the wake. This puts you in the right spot for having smooth, fun wake crossings.

Don't pop up too fast, stay low, be sure your board is on a plane, and try to keep your movements slow and steady.

Most of your weight will be on the elbows as the board starts to plane. Keeping the weight evenly on the elbows, start to pull your knees under you.

Move your knees into position on the edge of the pad and pull the strap over your knees into proper tightness and position.

Proper weight distribution: strap tight over the legs, back straight, shoulders rolled back. It all adds up to the correct body position.

WAKE JUMPING

Once you've mastered the basics of getting up and riding, which won't take long, you'll want to do something a little more challenging. A good first trick for kneeskiers is wake jumping. It's the building block for learning other tricks because it's *the* basic maneuver.

In wake jumping, timing is of the utmost importance. First, swing out to either side of the wake; make an easy turn into the wake, pointing the nose of your board into the wake. Don't make the mistake of leaning off the board. When you're making a left turn, shift your weight to the left so that the left rail will dig into the water.

As you head toward the wake on the edge of the board, keep your head up. Your arms should be in a normal skiing position, with your elbows lightly touching your PFD. To accelerate, lean away from the boat, but (as in slalom skiing) not necessarily back on the board. As you approach the wake, flatten your board out, ride to the crest of the wake and then spring, using the upper part of your body. When you feel the boat pull you, while still in the air, pull your arms in so that the board doesn't do a nosedive and you don't "go out the front!"

While you're in the air, keep your arms in and *look at the horizon!* Remember, if you look down, you fall down. For the smoothest wake jumps, you should clear both wakes at once. If

Make a weight shift in the direction you wish to go. You can even use your inside hand to help you turn and get the board on a sharp edge into the wake.

The opposite of skiing—flatten the board off at the bottom of the wake.

Pull your arms in at the height of the jump to keep the nose of the board up.

Hold your body position as the board makes contact with the water.

you are not doing this, you may need to speed up or shorten the rope to get all the way over both wakes.

Look for a spot about five feet in front of where you want to land instead of looking straight down, and your board's nose will stay up.

After you've mastered wake jumping, you'll undoubtedly want to move on to other tricks, such as the 180-degree turn and 360-degree turn as in traditional trick skiing. That's the fun of kneeboarding—it's a lot like trick skiing in that there is always something new to learn!

Many kneeboarders have been pushing new limits, and the sport has become so popular that they now have their own organization and their own competitions. To find out about the American Kneeboard Association (AKA), contact the American Water Ski Association.

The AKA sponsors novice and rated tournaments all across the country, with age-group divisions. For novice kneeskiers, competition is in turning—how many 360-degree turns one can complete in 20 seconds.

The novice wake jump event is designed to see how many times you can clear the wakes in twenty seconds.

SLALOM KNEEBOARDING

A kneeboarder graduates from novice competition to slalom events and tricks. Slalom kneeboarders use a regulation slalom course, but with an additional set of buoys halfway between the boat gates and the skier buoys. This allows competitors to go around either set of buoys, with varying amounts of points accumulated. (In the Open division, you are required to ski around the outside buoys.)

Trick competition offers two 20-second passes in which skiers attempt to do as many tricks as possible. Each trick has a predetermined point value, and the event is judged by five judges who remain on shore, similar to traditional trick skiing.

*World-Champion
Barefooter Ron Scarpa
shows perfect form.*

BAREFOOTING

Barefooters are the thrill seekers of the water-skiing world. You don't need a lot of equipment to get in on the fun. All you need is a boat, a rope, a good barefoot wetsuit, and your own two feet. There's nothing quite like the thrill of the first time you ride on top of the water on just the skin of your feet.

A barefoot wetsuit has a life vest actually sewn into the neoprene. The main reason for this is that a life vest worn over a wetsuit could catch water and bucket during falls. If the flotation is sewn in, the water flows over a smooth surface and there's no chance of bucketing or drag. Barefoot suits also have extra padding on the bottom and crotch areas since these sensitive areas take lots of abuse when barefooting. Most barefoot suits have either short sleeves or a tank-style top. This suit will be the biggest investment you make in barefooting, but trust me, all it takes is one bad spill in a swimsuit to convince you the cost is worth it.

Barefooters prefer a 100-foot rope, rather than the standard 70-foot rope. This is because there is less turbulence behind the boat at these lengths. Barefooters use ropes with as little stretch in them as possible, and if you get serious about the sport you may want to look into the Kevlar ropes designed specifically for barefooting. At the very least, you should look for a low-stretch polyethylene rope. The less stretch in the rope, the less chance for injury from losing or popping the handle and having it sling-shot into your foot or any other body part.

In addition to your barefoot wetsuit and 100-foot rope, you'll need a handle. Unless you plan to ski with your teeth like seventy-six-year-old "Banana" George Blair, you can probably get away with your regular handle. A single handle, not a double, is a must.

FIRST STEPS

One popular misconception about barefooting is that you go exceptionally fast. In fact, the average person can barefoot at 36 mph—the same speed for slalom skiing through the course. There is a simple formula for determining how fast you should go to barefoot: divide your weight by 10, then add 20; so, for example, a 160-pound man should go 36 mph.

As with all new water-skiing skills, it's a good idea to practice proper body position on dry land first. Your feet should be slightly ahead of your shoulders and about shoulder-width apart. Keep your knees bent and your back straight—almost like sitting in a chair—for the most stable position.

The easiest start method is with a kneeboard. To use a kneeboard for barefooting, you sit on the kneeboard, straddling it with your legs on either side. This position will be a little wobbly until you get a feel for it, so it's a help if your driver keeps the rope taut at all times. As is the case with any kind of water skiing, the driver can make learning how to barefoot easy or difficult. As the rope becomes tight, pull your legs out of the water from the straddle position and rest them on the nose of the board as the driver slowly accelerates to about 10 to 20 mph. Keep the handle in close to your waist. It may stabilize the board if you grip the edge of the nose of the kneeboard with your feet.

When the boat has accelerated almost up to your calculated speed, put your feet lightly on the water, in front of you, on either side of the nose of the kneeboard. Concentrate on flexing your feet up and turn your toes slightly in.

Signal your driver to accelerate slowly up to the appropriate speed. As the board begins to plane, shift your weight from the kneeboard onto your feet. The kneeboard will slip away as you put pressure on your feet, and you'll be barefooting before you know it.

There are some very important adjustments that can make the difference between a successful first attempt and a major face slam into the water. The first: *always keep your toes up!* All it takes to send you tumbling forward is to catch one toe.

Keep your arms straight, shoulders rolled back, and upper body strong. You should ski in a position that looks very much like sitting in a chair. Stay low, keep your knees bent, and keep those toes up.

Also, *do not dig your heels into the water*. The water should be breaking just below the balls of your feet, not slapping at your arches. This may not seem to make sense at first, but you want your feet to glide across the water. This is a minor adjustment that can really make a difference.

There are some common problems in learning this first kneeboard start. For example, if your kneeboard bounces wildly out of control, it's most likely that you're sitting back too far on it. If you adjust your position but the board still bounces, your driver may be at fault. Be sure the driver knows to accelerate *slowly and gradually* to allow enough time for you to plant your feet and feel comfortable.

If you try to plant your feet on the water in front of you and they keep getting pushed back, chances are you aren't bending your knees enough and keeping slight pressure there.

If you fall when the kneeboard slips away rather than shifting your weight onto your feet, your legs are definitely too straight. Remember, you should be in the "chair" position.

DROPPING OUT

If you don't have a kneeboard but own a slalom ski, you might want to learn barefooting by doing a step-off. It's very similar to learning to drop a ski when you go from combo skis to slalom, but with this you go from slalom to no skis. It's probably best to start out on a combo ski with an adjustable binding so that you can loosen the binding and let it slip off easily.

For a barefoot step-off start, you do things just slightly differently than when you drop a ski for slalom. Instead of staying inside the wake directly behind the boat, move toward the outside of the wake so that the back foot on your slalom ski will be next to the wake when you take it out and plant it for barefooting. (In other words, if you ski right foot forward, go outside the right wake, so that your left foot will be next to the wake.) The smooth water just under the curl of the wake is where you'll place your back foot when you're ready. This position helps keep the ski stable while you shift your weight onto your foot.

As your driver pulls you up to barefoot speed at about 25 mph you should start the step-off process. Check your body position. Make sure your arms are straight, shoulders rolled back, and knees well bent. Keep your weight over the ski but take your back foot out and place it on the water heel first, slightly in front of your other foot. It should be slightly in front of your shoulders, with your feet shoulder-width apart. Remember to keep your toes up!

Stay in this position until you feel comfortable with how your bare foot feels on the water, then signal the driver to accelerate to your computed speed. (Remember drivers, accelerate slowly and smoothly.) Maintain pressure on your bare foot on the water.

The barefoot boom sticks out from the side of the boat and is anchored to the nose of the boat for stability. Toehold barefooting is an advanced trick and should only be attempted with a qualified coach.

As the boat accelerates, gradually shift your weight to that foot, unweighting the foot in the ski.

When you have all your weight over the bare foot, point the toe of the foot still in the ski and lift that heel; the ski should slide away. Place this foot on the water, toes up, parallel to the other bare foot, then shift your weight slowly until it is evenly balanced over both feet.

Remember to keep your arms straight, shoulders rolled back, knees bent in the chair position, and toes up.

BOOMS

The easiest method for learning to barefoot is from a boom. Barefoot booms are specially designed poles, similar to a ballet barre, which are anchored to the center pylon of the boat. The boom protrudes off the side, perpendicular to the boat, and has a guidewire attached from the very end of the boom to the front of the bow for stability.

Contrary to appearance, booms are very safe if attached properly. If you fall from one you won't hit the boom because it will be moving away too fast. Neither will you hit or go under the boat if the boom is used with care and the accompanying instructions are closely followed.

Most barefoot schools use booms for instruction, but the cost of the boom (around $500) can be prohibitive to weekend skiers. Also, special care must be used in driving with a boom, as the extra weight, pull, and drag on one side of the boat can cause steering problems.

WHAT GOES UP MUST COME DOWN

Once you're actually barefooting you're probably going to wonder how to *stop*. When you are ready to stop simply stay in a sitting position and let go of the handle and lean back; you will gradually slide to a stop.

I guess I should forewarn you that some of the spills in barefooting can be rather sudden and not always fun. Not that one doesn't have bad falls in skiing, but in barefooting the falls seem to happen in a heartbeat. And it doesn't matter how competent a barefooter you are either. When I was seventeen I was barefooting for a video. Holding on to the boom at the side of the boat, I had my head turned to face a video camera and was talking into it when I suddenly caught a toe. Down I went, slamming the side of my face into the water. It wasn't until the next day that I realized the reason it was so painful and I couldn't hear well was that I burst my eardrum in the fall.

More commonly, barefooting falls lead to water going places you rather it didn't. That's why you need a protective wetsuit, with a well-padded seat! There are a few ways to lessen the severity of the falls you take. Don't resist the fall. If you feel yourself going down, tuck and roll. Let go of the handle when you fall forward. Once again, when you're ready to stop, just let go and sit back and slide.

There's something akin to a brotherhood or sisterhood among barefoot skiers, which is why there are so many enthusiasts. There are organized competitions for barefooting just as there are for us "stick skiers." The best way to learn more about competitions is to contact the American Barefoot Club through the American Water Ski Association.

Some of the events you'll see in competition include wake slalom (like slalom skiing), in which barefooters take two 15-second passes each to see who can cross the wakes the most times. Competitors ski this event both forwards and backwards, and can cross on two feet or with one held in the air. There is also trick barefooting, again with two 15-second passes. Performing in front of judges, barefooters do the same sort of tricks as water skiers, including front flips. And finally, believe it or not, there is barefoot jumping. The ramp is severely modified for the sport (18 inches high and 4 feet wide compared to 5 feet high and 14 feet wide for traditional skiing), although to me that doesn't make it any less frightening.

Once you've become proficient at barefoot basics, if you really want to progress, I would recommend attending one of the many fine barefoot schools now operating. A good instructor can do a lot for your self-confidence as well as your technique.

OTHER TOYS

Two other skiing toys that are starting to become popular deserve mention. The skiboard is a surfboard designed to be pulled behind a boat. Skiboarding is actually a lot like snowboarding. Until recently, skiboarding had been difficult to learn because, unlike surfboards, skiboards were bulky and made of foam-filled polyurethane plastic similar to the kneeboard. They were extremely buoyant and hard to control on the deep-water start. The recently introduced thinner, fiberglass model which is compression-molded like a slalom ski and is sure to capture the fancy of inland surfers and summertime snowboarders everywhere.

And the traditional tube will always remain popular with the younger set because it's easy to ride and easy to pull.

With any of these toys, it's important that the driver understands the nature of the toy and drives accordingly. And when you're pulling small children, keep a gentle touch.

QUICK TIPS

- Kneeboarding is a favorite sport for kids. It's easy to learn and speeds are slow.
- Begin kneeboarding with a beach start, then learn the deep-water start once you fall. Once you've mastered kneeboarding, it's easy to learn barefooting by first getting up on a kneeboard.
- Barefoot skiing requires only a rope, a boat, a barefoot suit, and your own two feet.
- Good body position is key to successful barefooting—back straight, shoulders rolled back, knees bent, feet flexed up, and toes pointed in.
- The easiest method for learning to start is a kneeboard or a boom if you have access to one.
- Learn more about barefooting or kneeboarding through the American Water Ski Association.
- Many of these toys have recommended towing speed limits and it's wise not to exceed them, especially when pulling children.

TEACHING
YOUR CHILD
TO WATER SKI

WHETHER THEY START with kneeboards, other toys, or "trainer" skis, kids can begin skiing at a very young age. I was just four years old my first time out. After practicing the basics on dry land with my father, the two of us took to the water. After a couple of tries, I successfully stood up on my skis on the water. This was the moment he'd been waiting for—his daughter was about to follow in his footsteps and fall in love with skiing. I, on the other hand, figured once I'd stood up and skied briefly, I'd mastered that trick. It became a contest of wills as I stubbornly threw down the handle to the rope and refused to ski. My father, proving he was more stubborn than I, eventually won out by leaving me floating in the middle of the lake for what seemed like an eternity. (I now suspect it was only about 10 minutes.)

I wouldn't recommend this particular method for teaching your child. But as your enthusiasm about water skiing increases, do think about teaching your child to ski. Water skiing is a great sport for the whole family to enjoy together, but it's a good idea to take things step by step.

First, and most important, your child should feel comfortable around the water. If you're a boating enthusiast, take your children on excursions so that being on the water will seem entirely natural to them. The loud roar and unsteady motion of a boat on the water can be frightening at first. One good way to acclimate a very small child to the boat is by having him sit in a carseat that is securely fastened in the boat initially. And older children will feel more at home on board if you teach them all about the boat and how it works.

Learning to swim is one of the great joys of childhood, and it is the best way to increase your child's confidence around water. Teach your child to swim at whatever age you think is appropriate—or take advantage of one of the many programs that exist even for very young children. Once this basic water skill is mastered, both of you will feel more relaxed and comfortable about moving on to skiing. (It is a good idea to have children wear life vests when boating, even if they know how to swim. It's the law in many states.)

If you have kids, you know how eager they are to absorb knowledge about almost anything and to learn new skills—especially when it's something you're enthusiastic about. The drama, excitement, and just plain *fun* of water skiing are sure to capture their imaginations.

EQUIPMENT

Many avid skiers start their children at very young ages (three or four). This can be successful if one approaches the subject with care—and the right equipment.

First and most important, get a Coast Guard–approved PFD that fits snugly on your child. Don't buy one that they'll grow into; buy one that fits them now, so that they'll be safe *now*. If your child is very small, under 40 pounds, you may want to purchase a pair of "trainer" skis. These are about half the size of regular combination skis and are tied together with a few inches of rope at the front and back of the skis so they won't separate. The skis are designed so that although the child holds on to a rope handle, the rope bridle that is actually attached to the boat threads through the front-cross stability rope, which means that the pull comes from the skis, not the child's arms; the boat literally pulls the skis along. Several companies now produce these skis, but our experience has been that some are too narrow. Be sure the pair you purchase are wide and flat, for added stability.

A regular ski rope is fine, but you'll want to make sure you've

Have fun in the learning stages. Practice proper body position and "ski" across the grass.

got a handle with an extra-small grip. A single-handle rope is by far preferable to the old-fashioned two-handle style. If you have a slalom-style rope with loops that can be easily shortened, this can be very helpful. Pulling a child at a 45- or 60-foot length is a good starting point; the rope is less likely to sag and drag in the water at the slow speeds you'll be going. (Some people even recommend holding the rope in your hands when starting with the tied-together trainer skis or using a trick-release mechanism. This way, you can release the rope as soon as a child falls, ensuring they'll remain unharmed even if they don't pop out of their ski bindings and the boat keeps pulling the skis along. I've used this method successfully.)

FOUNDATION

To lay a good foundation for your on-the-water instruction you should start on dry land as with all ski techniques. Familiarize your child with the skis, teaching him how to put them on and take them off. Have him learn how to buckle his own vest. Make a game of it. When he has on a pair of skis, playfully pull him across a rug or the grass. This will teach him what skiing feels like before he ever gets in the water.

Here I am at six years old really making spray!

The more comfortable the child becomes, the more instruction you can offer. Teach a proper stance from the beginning—knees bent, back straight, shoulders rolled back, and arms straight. Have her squat down on the skis, with knees bent and back straight, arms extended and hands holding the ski rope handle. Pull her up from this position, always reminding her to keep her shoulders back. Keep in mind that children have very short attention spans. If you can play "water ski" for 15 minutes at a time, you'll be doing great.

Gradually move your ski play closer to the water. Try pulling your child up and along the shore of the lake in shallow water.

Once the child feels comfortable with the equipment and you've stimulated the child's interest in skiing, it's time to get wet.

There are a variety of methods for teaching a child in the water. One that works particularly well with parents or teachers who are accomplished skiers is to actually ski with the child on your pair of skis.

There is one prerequisite for this method that is of utmost importance: *you must be an excellent skier yourself*. If you're not

yet steady enough to slalom ski, don't try combo skiing with a child. The potential for getting hurt is too great.

Make sure that you both wear good-quality, Coast Guard–approved life vests if you decide to attempt this. Similar to teaching a child to dance by having him stand on your feet, skiing with a child on your skis gives the child the sensation of skiing without the fear. He'll be able to understand what it's supposed to feel like, so that when he attempts it on his own it's not such a bewildering experience.

If the child is small enough, you can hold him in your arms. With a large child put him on the front of your skis and have him place his feet just in front of the bindings and hands on the handle. Wrap your arms securely around him and take off and

Assuming you can ski at the speed the child needs to go, a fun way to teach your child to ski is beside her. You're close enough to help correct any problems and it gives the child an extra added amount of security.

ski as you normally would. One caveat: don't have the driver pull you too fast. If you can plane off, 18 or 20 mph is probably safest.

If you're not comfortable taking your child on your own skis, then try skiing beside him. This requires two ropes, and you'll have to be especially careful not to spray him with your skis. Also, if you've got a very small child, this method won't work because the boat must go at his speed, not yours.

Another method that works well with an older child is to stand out in the shallow water and balance the child in the starting position, reassuring him that the boat will come right back to pick him up if he falls. Start the child in fairly shallow water, if possible, so you're able to stand nearby and steady him in position until the boat takes off, eliminating the floundering around until starting off.

DRIVING FOR CHILDREN

One of the biggest mistakes made by family instructors is driving the boat too fast. A father takes his son skiing behind a bass boat and has no conception of the proper speed. The child hangs on for dear life, trying his best to stay up, but he's bent forward and ready to wipe out at any minute as his father blissfully speeds along at 25 mph. This is all too common a scenario.

When teaching children, remember: *the slower, the better!* For very young children, from four to six, you don't need to go more than idle speed on most boats to give them all the pull they'll need to get up. Even older children, at ten to twelve, probably won't need to be pulled at more than 15 mph. This may seem incredibly slow to you, but to their small and lightweight bodies, it's just the right amount of pull.

The driver plays a critical role in the success or failure of any new skier. If he punches it and tries to pull a skier too quickly, the driver will probably cause him to fall. When learning, some kids will ski for quite some time squatting on their skis before they ever stand up. The driver must pull them steadily and slowly in order for them to succeed. Accelerate gradually until they're on a plane. If the child starts to lean forward and lock his knees, you may be going too fast. Try slowing down a little and signal to him to keep his shoulders back and his knees bent.

It's important to remind your child to let go of the rope as soon as he falls.

SET AN EXAMPLE

If your child is enthusiastic about his experience, he'll be watching you intently for clues on how to improve. For this reason, it's vital that you obey the rules of skiing etiquette and boat driving at all times.

In fact, a good way to teach a child responsibility is to have him observe while you ski. Tell him to translate your signals to the driver, and then you can teach him what the universal skier's signals are (thumbs up for "faster," thumbs down for "slower," a pat on the head for "head home," hand slicing across the throat for "cut"). He'll pick up these signals in no time and you'll be surprised when he starts telling you what to do while he skis.

Another point to teach your young observer is to use the word *fall* to tell the driver a skier is down. Often the driver is concentrating on keeping a steady speed, and when an observer says "uh oh," or "oops," the driver doesn't pay any attention. If you say "down" the driver may think you mean slow down. If you say simply "fall," it immediately conveys what the driver needs to do. And if the habit is started young, it will stay with your child.

MOVING ON

You'll probably want to start your child on trainer skis that are tied together. As mentioned, the towrope can be attached to the skis so that the child holds the handle, but the boat is actually pulling from the center stabilizer rope on the skis. Once the child is comfortable getting up and staying up on the skis, the next step is to change the rope so that he'll be holding it himself and feel the pull of the boat.

Most kids master the training skis fairly quickly. If you have an older child (eight to ten years old), you may want to just start on a beginner's pair of combination skis.

Whatever you choose to do, your child will probably progress fairly quickly and will be ready for "adult" skis before you realize it. Don't rush him too much though. When a child is comfortable on two skis directly behind the boat, you should encourage him to learn to cross the wakes. This technique is the same as for adults.

Wake crossing is a big hurdle for a child to overcome. Although it's easy to do once you know how, it can seem impossible until you've tried it once—especially if you're only four feet tall! So make a big deal of it when your child succeeds.

When a child has mastered crossing both wakes with ease, he'll probably begin to get bored. Then he'll be ready to move on to slalom skiing. If you have a beginner's pair of combo skis, it's easy to teach your child to ski on one ski.

Again, return to the shore for the same fundamentals as you would with an adult. Teach your child to slalom ski by first dropping a ski. The difficult part of this method is learning to keep the weight on one leg while moving the other. However, this is much easier for children to learn than adults. Don't be surprised when your child surpasses you in skiing ability.

In no time at all, your child should be able to ski on one ski. If he has trouble, you may want to ski beside him and support him by holding on to one shoulder or arm while he drops a ski.

If the child shows a real affinity for the sport and a natural athleticism, it might be time to investigate the possibility of professional instruction. There are a large number of qualified instructors with ski schools, many of whom have coached world champions. As with any sport, it's always best to learn proper technique in the beginning.

For more information about water skiing and skiing instruction, contact the American Water Ski Association, 799 Overlook Drive SE, Winter Haven, FL 33884-1671; 813-324-4341.

A word of caution: be sure your child is mentally ready. If you force the child, he may hate a sport he would have otherwise loved. You can bet your bathing suit that my young son, Alexander, won't be made to ski until he's ready. Remember, this is supposed to be fun.

QUICK TIPS

- For small children, you may want to use trainer skis that are tied together. Also, you may want to shorten the tow-rope length, and for very small children the observer may hold the rope in his hand so he can release it immediately if the child falls or use a trick release.
- Children are quick to learn new skills, but their attention span is short. Start on dry land and learn body position, and make a game of "skiing" by pulling them across grass on the skis.
- Be sure to have the proper equipment, especially a PFD that fits the child snugly.
- Children can be taught a number of ways: by starting in shallow water, by skiing on your skis with you (only if you're a competent skier yourself), or by having you ski beside them.
- The number one mistake people make when trying to teach children is driving the boat too fast. Some children can pop up and ski at idle speed. When driving for children, remember, the slower the better, but not so slow that the child is sinking or working to stay up.
- Set a good example when you ski: use proper safety equipment, use hand signals, and be courteous to others.

T E N

CROSSING THE LINE— SKIING YOUR FIRST TOURNAMENT

IF **YOU CAN** get around any of the buoys of a slalom course or perform even a few tricks or ride successfully away from a jump, you're ready to ski in your first tournament. I'm not kidding. At the novice level, everyone is a beginner, so you have no excuses.

FIRST THINGS FIRST

First, you need to join the American Water Ski Association (AWSA). For $35 you can become a competing member, and you will automatically be covered by their $1 million liability insurance (to cover injuries in tournaments). You'll receive a rule book, a subscription to their magazine, and be eligible to ski in tournaments. (AWSA, 799 Overlook Drive SE, Winter Haven, FL 33884-1671; 813-324-4341.)

AWSA water ski tournaments are divided into categories designed to encourage new skiers to improve their skill levels at their own pace. As a novice, you'll be eligible to ski in novice-only tournaments where you will compete only against people in your age group and of the same sex. Everyone there will be at about the same skill level, and for most it will be their first competition, so you needn't worry about some pro ringer crashing your event. AWSA ensures this through a national rating system based on skill level. Once you've passed a certain skill level, you are no longer eligible for novice tournaments but must move up to the next division. Many tournaments set up for national rankings will have novice age groups as well as national-level competition.

The U.S. is divided by AWSA into five regions. AWSA can tell you how to obtain a copy of your Regional Guide. These handy publications list all the tournaments in your region as well as give helpful information about the tournament sites, hotels in the area, directions, and so forth.

Since many sites are primitive at best, it's a good idea to pack a cooler with water and light snacks such as fruit and yogurt, and take along some lawn chairs. Eat a light breakfast the morning of your tournament, if you can, at least an hour before your event. Save the sandwiches and heavier foods until after you've skied.

THE EVENT

I know one of the most intimidating aspects of competition can be what to expect at one's first event. So I'm going to outline an average tournament for you.

When you register for or enter a tournament, you should be given directions to the site and a schedule of events. Get there in plenty of time before the tournament begins. When you arrive, you'll need to find the registration area and check in. You'll be required to show your AWSA card and sign a ski club safety release. You may also be asked to fill out a biographical form so the site announcer will know a little about you when you are on the course. The skier starting list and the judges are also located at the registration area, and this is where scores will be posted once the events get under way.

If the tournament is scheduled to start at 8:30 A.M., and your event is later, you should still be there close to starting time. Events run consecutively, so if a few skiers don't show up, your event may take place earlier than expected. If you're really concerned about this, you can call the tournament director close to the date of the event and find out how many people are scheduled to ski before you.

A good rule of thumb is that a slalom ride will take seven minutes, a jump or trick ride, five minutes. Of course, in a novice tournament, where people might miss or fall on their first pass, these times may not apply.

If you miss your event, you'll be scratched from that event only, and probably not eliminated from the entire tournament.

When you arrive, find out where the starting dock is located. I try to be at the dock about 20 minutes before I ski; I don't want to feel rushed putting on my equipment. You are allowed to bring your own handle, and obviously you'll need your ski. You'll also need an approved life vest and gloves. An official will conduct a safety check of your equipment before you're allowed to ski. They are looking for sharp edges or loose screws on your ski, or anything dangerous about your equipment. They'll measure the length of your handle on a measuring board device with a weight that simulates pull to make sure the handle is within tolerance. This is a very important point. Once I had a handle on which the bridle was one centimeter longer than tolerance, and the officials wouldn't allow it, because it gives a skier an unfair advantage to have a longer rope.

If your handle is too long, here's a little tip: don't tie a knot in the rope to shorten it because it will break. Instead, take a pencil or twig and feed it through the center of the rope, so that none of it sticks out. It will expand the rope and will usually shorten it enough to be within tolerance. You can ski with it inside your rope. I've done this dozens of times to make my handle the correct length—it's a great quick fix at the tournament. Most of the time the handles come the correct length from the manufacturer. But sometimes, if they are worn, they can be stretched out of tolerance.

Do your stretching and limbering up before you ski. Keep in mind you only have one shot at the course. If you miss a buoy or fall your score ends, so you want your muscles to be ready. Also, you need to feel ready mentally. You can do this as you watch the skiers before you. It's a good idea to note where the boat turns, where the skiers pull out to start, and anything else that will help you know what to expect when you get on the water. Another way to give yourself an edge is to note the scores of the other skiers. It will give you something to shoot for. How-

Feed a pencil or twig of similar diameter inside the braids of the line. When it's fully inserted it will generally shorten your line enough to be within tolerances.

ever, don't let the other scores pressure you into forgetting about your own technique. *That* should be your number-one concern. When the skier or two before you is ready to go, start putting on your gear. I try to be ready by the time the person in front of me jumps in the water, just in case they fall early.

If you feel nervous, try some visualization. See yourself doing everything perfectly. If you visualize yourself falling, start over and visualize yourself skiing perfectly. (I do this before I get out of bed on the day of the tournament.)

The starter on the dock will call your name and tell you when to get in the water. The boat will swing around to get you, and at this point the dock starter will change handles for you. There will be three people in the boat: a timer, a judge, and a driver. This same crew will officiate for everyone in your division. No friends, family, or coaches are allowed.

The timer is there to time the boat through the course. This is done on every pass, so the speed will be accurate and fair for everyone. The boat judge is there to count buoys and to make sure that you go through the gates. Also he looks for unfair conditions such as rough water.

For slalom, before you start your run, the boat judge will ask you what speed and rope length you want to start at. As you get more experienced in competition, you'll find it may be best to start a run slower than you do at home, as the ski site is unfamiliar to you. The slower speed will give you a better margin for error.

INTO THE WATER YOU GO

Basically, you ski until you either fall or can't make it around a buoy. If you fall, signal immediately that you're okay. There will either be a pickup boat, or you'll have to swim to shore. If you don't fall but miss a buoy, they'll turn around and take you back to the starting dock, but not through the course. You'll find your score or the total number of buoys posted at the registration area.

One quick note about rerides: if something causes you to fall or miss a buoy on your pass and if the judge deems the conditions unfair, you'll be offered a reride. This will be indicated by a flag, as explained in the AWSA rules, or the driver will stop the boat and the judge will explain it to you. If you didn't make the pass you may want to take the reride. But if it's your best score, keep it. Don't give it away unless you are positive you can do better. If you've skied all six buoys and are still offered a reride based on rough water or fast speed, you're not obligated to take it. Keep those six buoys!

If you don't understand the signal or flag, ask the judge to explain it to you.

The basic starting dock etiquette is the same for slalom, jump, and tricks. Arrive before your turn to ski and be ready to ski as soon as the skier before you has begun his run. Be sure to inquire about starting dock location changes because sometimes they are in different places for different events.

For trick ski competition remember you'll get two twenty-second passes. You'll be asked to write down at registration what tricks you plan to do (your dream sheet), and you'll be expected to stick to the exact order in which you've written them. For trick skiing, the rules allow you to have someone you trust ride in the boat to handle the release. Be sure to inform the boat judge of your preferred speed. The passes are run consecutively without stopping, so if you like different speeds for your run, the time to tell the driver is before you leave the dock. Remember, each boat speed is calibrated a little differently and if at any time the speed doesn't feel right you may direct the driver to go faster or slower with the thumbs-up or thumbs-down signal relayed by the judge.

When you have the correct speed, indicate to the judge it's okay. Most judges will get your attention once the speed is set and give you an okay signal; if the speed feels good signal okay or nod your head.

After you've skied, your score will be announced and written down at the registration area. If you would like to know how the judges arrived at your score, you can ask the scorer to see your trick sheets and the five judges' forms will be given to you. It's a good idea to check your trick sheets after every tournament so you will know what tricks you weren't given credit for and what to work on for next time. If you don't understand something, ask. The judges are very friendly and will take time out, if they have it, to answer your questions.

For jumping competition, the start dock area is basically the same as for slalom. According to AWSA Safety Rules, you'll have to wear a helmet. You should be prepared to tell the driver both the speed you want and where you want the boat to go in relation to the jump ramp. (Your jump coach will be able to help with this.) Once you take off from the dock, the boat will go down, turn, and start back toward the ramp. Strive for your usual setup for the jump—double cut, etc. One word of caution: each jump ramp feels a little different, so on the first of your three allotted jumps, take it a little easy if you are at the cutting stage. Once you get a feel for the ramp, then you can add some aggressive cuts. After you land and ski away, the judge in the boat will signal your score. After your three jumps you will be returned to the start dock.

MENTAL PREPARATION

Preparing yourself mentally for a tournament should feel a lot like preparing yourself for practice. I see so many regional and national-level skiers go out and ski practice runs without concentrating on improving their mental skills; they then find themselves mentally unprepared when it comes time to compete. To improve your skiing scores you must set specific goals for yourself on a month-to-month basis and even on a set-to-set basis. For instance, one of the things I hold myself up to is that when I practice I know I want to ski my 35 off pass twice. I also require myself to run my warm-up passes without falling or missing gates or buoys. So when I go out to practice, I really have a competition mindset. By putting that kind of mental pressure on yourself you'll be used to it before you ever get to an event, and this will drastically cut down on your nerves. I still remember the vivid verbal pictures my coach Liz Allen used to paint for me in practice. Just before I got into the water, she would say, "Here we are at the World Championships, so and so has just run X number of buoys and Camille needs that plus two to win the competition and bring home the team title." Talk about sweating bullets! But that kind of pressure made me really consistent. Training this way gives you a mental edge when you go to a tournament because you know you can run your passes every time. After all, you've run them consistently in practice.

I also train myself mentally with visualization. The morning of a tournament, before I put my feet on the floor, I visualize myself making perfect runs with emphasis on technique, all the way through to what my personal best is in practice. I feel this is very important, because visualizing something you've done successfully is a great way of reinforcing it in your mind. If you're a 22 off skier, it won't do you any good to visualize yourself running 41 off because you haven't experienced it. That's just daydreaming, not visualizing!

The more you work with this type of visualization, especially when you do it on a day-to-day basis, you'll actually begin to feel your muscles contracting at the appropriate times while you're mentally seeing your runs.

This technique may or may not work for you the morning of the tournament. You may find it easier to do it when you're at the tournament site and can hear the sound of the boat.

Another mental preparation technique that some skiers use is to go off and sit by themselves just before their run, listening on their Walkman to music that gets them psyched up, or just meditating. Other skiers find it easier to have conversations and pretend the tournament is just another, normal, relaxed day of skiing. Through trial and error you will find what works best for you.

PHYSICAL PREPARATION

While mental preparation is an individual thing, there are some specific guidelines to help you prepare physically for a tournament. When you know you're going to ski in a competition on the weekend, you should have done all your hard practice and technique adjustment two or three weeks prior to the date of the event. The last three weeks before the event should be repetitive rehearsal, devoted to polishing your technique, not making radical style changes, or changing skis.

You must set a goal for yourself, a realistic score and have a battle plan. On the Monday before the competition, ski hard. If you're only skiing slalom, such a practice might consist of two hard rounds with some back-to-back passes at the same rope length, really concentrating on your style and technique. This will reinforce your confidence when you're in the heat of competition and make your technique mere muscle memory.

On Tuesday, you should follow the same guidelines. But on Wednesday, switch to a light training session. If you've been skiing two rounds, only ski one. On Thursday, you may be traveling, but try to do one round as if it were the tournament, kind of like a rehearsal. Start at the speed you will ski in the tournament and run until you miss. On Friday, take the day off and rest your body. You won't forget how to run the course between Thursday and Saturday, no matter how nervous you are. In fact, you'll be surprised at how much stronger you'll feel if you let your body rest for a day. On Saturday, you'll be ready for your first round of competition.

ONCE YOU GET THERE

Keep in mind that each site is different. Conditions to be aware of include:

- longer or shorter boat lineup than at your home site
- different boat
- different driver
- different water consistency (Believe it or not, you will be able to tell a difference between hard and soft water.)
- wind conditions—backwash or rough water in certain areas

It's a good idea to watch what the other skiers are doing— unless, of course, you're first out. It gives you some idea of what the setup is like. Keep in mind that all boats and drivers are certified by AWSA, so this really shouldn't be a variable.

You should be aware of the wind conditions and have trained in a variety of them. Note the areas of backwash and be prepared to use your knees as shock absorbers to help lessen this effect. But above all, remember that you know how to ski, and try not to let these variables disrupt your concentration. Just get out there and ski like you know how. Stay focused, positive, and mentally strong.

BEFORE YOU LEAVE

After you have skied in a tournament, be sure to ask for a rating card, which will be available from the chief judge or the registrar. You need to fill it out and get it signed in order to have your score recorded and gain a higher rating. This is how you move up the ranks, so don't forget.

OFF SEASON

Most people don't live in a climate where they can ski on a year-round basis. Even pro skiers who live in Florida give themselves a couple of months off in the winter.

The bulk of competitions are held in June, July, and August. If you have a wetsuit, you can start training in May and extend your season as long as your climate allows. Before the season and at the end of the season are the best times to work on your technique, adjust your skis, change equipment, or deal with anything that affects how you ski. Once you're in the season, it's best to work with what you have and not make radical changes.

The off-season is a good time to get yourself in really good physical condition, which is the key to keeping your injuries low and performances high during the season. If you happen to live in one of the areas where you can't ski year-round, it's a good idea to go to a gym. You know from the first rounds of skiing each year which muscles get sore, so concentrate on them in the gym.

A lot of pro skiers are competitive in other sports. Many skiers play tennis, golf, snow ski, and bike race, not only because these sports are physical but because they like the mental challenge. Use your recreational time at these other sports to hone your mental skills.

Although skiing is an anaerobic sport, aerobics classes will give you an edge because they not only work your aerobic capacity but also build strength and flexibility. Aerobics also helps burn fat, if you need to lose a few extra pounds.

If you just can't stand being off all winter, you might look into some of the ski schools that operate in a warm climate. Keep in mind that if you go in winter, you won't have skied for a while, so really use the time in the gym. I recommend, to learn the most, to go after you have skied a few weeks and are over those beginning aches and pains. Another alternative is to go in the fall when you are strong and can really put a good coach's advice to use. Ski school will really turn your skiing up a notch. For a list of ski schools, contact the AWSA, 799 Overlook Drive SE, Winter Haven, FL 33884.

NUTRITION

Every athlete should be aware of good nutrition. Eating properly will enhance your performance. A diet balancing carbohydrates and protein, with less than 20 percent fat, is recommended by most doctors. This becomes ever more important when you get into competition. For instance, you don't want to have coffee and sugar-coated doughnuts the morning of your competition.

A good nutritional analogy is, the food you put into your body is like the gas you put into your car. The better the gas, the better performance you can expect from your car. High octane foods are skinless white meat chicken, fish, pasta for carbohydrates, whole wheat breads and grains, and lots of fresh vegetables. Avoid fatty foods that leave you feeling heavy and sluggish, and you'll perform better.

ABOVE ALL, CONCENTRATE— BE AGGRESSIVE AND BELIEVE IN YOURSELF

Concentration, aggressiveness, and confidence have always been key for me. The memory that stands out in my mind of putting this key to work is the U.S. Nationals in 1973 in Petersburg, Virginia. The year before I had skied well but had lost a gold medal because of a bad judging call. This was the year I wanted to make up for it.

At the Nationals, I went out in the slalom event and broke the record for thirteen-and-under girls, but so did another girl. I won the run-off and became the National Champion, but we remained co-record holders.

In the trick event I also broke the thirteen-and-under record and tied with the same girl. She won the run-off, but we remained co-record holders.

So it came down to the jumping event to see who would be the new National Overall Champion in our age division.

The week prior to the Nationals I had broken the jump record with an 87-foot jump, so I was primed. The same girl was out before me and jumped 90 feet! She had set a new national record!

I remember sitting in the water, waiting for my turn, and hearing the announcer say she had won the jump event and was the new National Overall Champion. I looked at the boat judge, who remembers to this day the look on my face. I said, "What the hell are they talking about, I haven't even skied yet! Let's go!" I promptly went out and jumped 94 feet for another national record, snatching the Overall title from her grasp. That jump record stood for twelve years.

I looked up on shore and saw my father and my coach, Chuck Dees, standing on a picnic table. When they announced my distance Chuck leapt off of the table in celebration. This left the table totally unbalanced and my dad was unceremoniously dumped onto the ground. What a sight! Tournament experiences can leave you with a lot of precious—sometimes humorous—memories.

QUICK TIPS

- To compete, you must become a member of the American Water Ski Association.
- You're ready to compete when you can get around any of the buoys in the slalom course, complete any tricks, or go over the jump ramp.

- AWSA offers novice-only tournaments, available in five regions across the country.
- Arrive early at the tournament site.
- Find registration and complete any paperwork.
- Locate the starting dock for your event and plan to be there 20 minutes before your start time.
- You must bring your own handle, approved PFD, and equipment. Officials will check equipment for safety before you ski.
- Stretch and limber up before you ski.
- At the site, check the pattern of skiers before you ski, look for backwash and check wind conditions. Familiarize yourself with the site.
- Mentally prepare for competition by creating tournament pressure in practice.
- Use visualization techniques to improve your performance.
- Physically prepare by setting goals for practice. Train in all wind conditions. Take at least one day off before a tournament.
- Eat lightly before a tournament and take light snacks and plenty of water.
- Concentrate, be aggressive, and believe in yourself.

ELEVEN

A SPECTATOR'S GUIDE TO WATER SKIING

I HOPE THIS BOOK will inspire you to attend some professional water-ski events, or at least watch them on TV. Watching professional skiing, just as watching other professional sports, is not only exciting, it can give you insight into your own skills and techniques. You may even find a role model or two.

Unlike amateur events, professional events have an exact starting time and finish time, generally around noon to 4:00 P.M. They're not all-day affairs because there aren't a large number of skiers competing. The qualifications to get into the first round of a pro event are very high, and at each round of competition, there's a fixed number of competitors. At a pro event, you'll be seeing the very best.

You'll probably have to pay an admission fee, just like in other pro sports, to get in to the tournament. Colorful banners representing sponsors will greet you. On-site, there will also be a mini-mall of water-ski industry products: ski boat displays, ski companies selling their wares and clothing. This can be a great opportunity to get a good buy on equipment that may not have reached the other skiers on your lake. And a lot of ski companies have autograph sessions with your favorite pro skiers, giving you an opportunity to meet and talk to them.

Throughout the tournament, an announcer describes what's going on in the competition. Usually he can be heard all across the site, so you can keep up with what's going on even if you're in a crowd.

The format of events at a pro tournament is a little different from what you'll see at an amateur competition. (You'll be able to pick up a program that explains the competition format.) Although jumping events are like those at amateur competitions, in slalom you may see what's called "head-to-head competition." These are generally held during the final round (usually on Sunday), providing a terrific climax to a weekend of skiing.

In head-to-head competition, the skiers first compete in elimination rounds, skiing straight up slalom, each skier competing against every other skier. These rounds narrow the field to the top four slalom skiers. In head-to-head, the skiers are seeded according to their performance up to that point. The best skier is pitted against the worst (one against four) and the number two skier goes against the number three skier. The winners of these two rounds will go head-to-head for the final victory.

What makes head-to-head competition so fast and exciting is that there are two boats on the water at the same time. As soon as one skier finishes his pass, the next skier starts his from the same end of the course on the same rope length. Strategy plays a big part in head-to-head slalom, adding second-by-second excitement. For spectators, head-to-head is a wonderful opportunity to compare different styles. The winner is determined immediately, based on the number of buoys each skier made.

Trick skiing in pro competition has each competitor making two 20-second passes, just as in amateur competition. But because there is only one judge, scores are instantaneously recorded on the scoreboard as soon as a pass is completed. Recently, the members of PAWS reassigned point values to old tricks and added new tricks for PAWS competitions. Now, the values for the most difficult tricks are higher, and you'll see a greater variety of the more exciting tricks, such as flips, as skiers try to up their scores.

Keep in mind that each tournament is important to the skiers. Every placement in every event counts toward the year-end ranking, as in tennis. The skier with the most Grand Prix points is named as the World Pro Champion for that year. The competition at the end of the year is hot and heavy. It's a phenomenon

I'm really familiar with—working hard to win the Women's World Pro title five years running!

Water-skiing events have been broadcast on TV for a long time. In 1977, the U.S. Team Trials, which selects the best six skiers in the country to compete for the U.S. team in world competition were covered by PBS on tape delay—and it was a good thing for me that it *was* tape delayed.

There I was, competing in the tricks event. And, like all skiers in a tricks event, I wasn't wearing a PFD—so I'd have maximum freedom of movement.

I took off from the dock and was doing a simple trick to set the boat speed when the driver turned the boat unexpectedly and I fell. Under international rules (which govern Team Trial competitions), I was penalized for falling by losing my first pass. What a disaster!

So the run wouldn't be a total loss, I knew I needed to kick into high gear and try to get in a few extra tricks. I was really smoking through my run when I felt the top of my bikini give. I finished the trick and looked down just as my top flew off!

I didn't know quite what to do, but I really wanted to make

the team even if I had to do it naked. I did three more tricks and fell because I was laughing so hard.

I remember surfacing and looking to the shore to see my father rolling on the ground with laughter. What a way to break the tension of an important tournament!

I looked at my trick sheets later and one judge had jokingly given me 1,000 bonus points for a trick called "boobs flying." Needless to say, even though the tournament was shown on educational television, my special trick was edited out.

In 1990, live coverage of water skiing competition made its television debut. The two-hour format covered all six events. This was an important milestone for the sport: live action offers a great behind-the-scenes look at an event, something often missing from the fast-paced taped shows.

A taped event is usually broadcast in a one-hour format. You see only the last pass or two of the finals in slalom, so it some-times looks as if the skier comes out and only made two buoys. In fact, they have made all the other passes prior to that one, so keep that in mind the next time you watch. Also, you won't see all three jumps for each competitor, nor will you see all trick passes. As a result, you have to rely on the commentator to tell you the full story of the tournament.

Watching water skiing on TV will undoubtedly whet your appetite for attending a pro event. If there's one in your area, it's a fantastic way for the family to spend a summer afternoon. You'll all enjoy the excitement of the crowd, and the skiers among you will see more great skiing than the limited TV coverage allows. And the more good skiing you see, the more you'll learn.

Stop by and see me next time you're there.

GLOSSARY

Appointed judge: Tournament official with judge's rating invited to administer a tournament at the direction of the Chief Judge.

Apron: Slanted safety side of a jump ramp; provides protection for when a jumper has cut too late or is out of control. *See also* Side curtain.

Arm sling: Harness used by jumpers to hold the arm close to the body and thus maintain body position against the force of the skier's pull away from the towboat.

AWSA: American Water Ski Association; the governing and sanctioning body for organized, amateur water skiing in the United States.

Backwash: Rough water resulting from boat wakes rebounding off fixed objects such as a boat, jump ramp, steep shoreline, or sea wall.

Balk: A jumper's refusal on approach to the ramp, accompanied by his release of the handle and his skiing past or over the left side of the ramp. A refusal with skier holding the handle and passing the ramp on the right is considered grounds for disqualification under the official rules.

Ball: *See* Buoy.

Bear trap: Toe strap used by trick skiers to close on the foot for toehold maneuvers.

Bevel: The sides of the ski, shaped into different angles to achieve specific performance characteristics. Bevels aid the skier in changing edge and stabilizing it in the approaching turn. They are considered "sharp" when the top and bottom edges of the ski have two distinct corners. Rounded bevels may have no discernible edge. Wide, flat bevels cause lift and may be found any place on the side of the ski. Variable bevels mean the shape of the edges change from front to tail.

Binding: Rubber boot mounting for the foot on the ski.

Bion: A high-tech stretchy breathable material developed for medical uses now used in wetsuits for freedom of movement.

Blade: *See* Fin.

Blank: Ski without a binding or fin.

Boat judge: Tournament official assigned to ride in the towboat with the driver for scoring, and to watch for unfair conditions.

Boom: An aluminum bar that attaches to the center pylon of a towboat and extends out the side opposite the driver. Booms are used to learn barefooting as well as regular skiing.

Bridle: Y-shaped 5-foot rope portion of handle attachment.

Buoy: Round or spherical marker used to indicate paths for skier and towboat in slalom and to outline limits in tricks and jump course. Usually orange and yellow, made of plastic and 9 inches in diameter.

Carbon graphite: Material used in some skis for stiffer flex and durability. *See* Graphite.

Ceramic: An off-white colored ski construction material that retains great strength and flexibility and is noted for its vibration-dampening qualities.

Compression-molded: Epoxy/fiberglass skis are composed of a polyure-thane foam core, a complete wrapping of fiberglass around the core, and a top skin of ABS plastic or aluminum. They are then "cooked" with heat and compressed for added strength.

Concave: Bottom configuration of a slalom ski for improved tracking in high-speed turns around buoys.

Counter cut: A jumper's maneuver from the left side of the boat wake to the right side in preparation for the crack-the-whip style cut to the ramp.

Course: Portion of a body of water, marked by buoys, where each event of water ski competition takes place.

Crash: A fall in jumping.

Crush: The involuntary bending of a jumper's knees on the ramp as a result of the G-force applied when the skis of the speeding skier hit the inclined surface. Opposite of spring.

Cut: Putting ski or skis on edge and pulling away from the force of the towboat.

Division: Age and/or sex category in competitive water skiing.

Double-cut: Crack-the-whip maneuver by a jumper to gain added speed on the approach to the ramp. *See* Counter cut.

Driver: The operator of a towboat in water ski competition who has been rated under qualifications established by AWSA. (Also the person operating a boat for recreational skiing.)

Early: Term used to describe the skier's correct position in the slalom course, in relation to the buoy. Also used to describe the timing of a jumper's cut toward the ramp.

Edge: (Verb) To hold a ski or skis on edge against the pull of the towboat to increase acceleration, or with the pull of the boat to decelerate. (Noun) The side, or bevel, of the ski.

Event: One of three disciplines in competitive water skiing and one of four disciplines in barefoot tournaments.

Fiberglass wrap: A total shell around the core of a ski, formed by a fitted piece of chopped fabriclike mat. The seam is located under the top of the ski.

Fin: Appendage on the bottom rear of a ski to make it track in the water. Also, appendage on the bottom of a towboat installed for lateral stabilization.

Flex: How much a ski will bend under pressure.

Freestyling: Style of skiing performed in ski shows, off the jump ramp; includes moves such as mule kicks, flips, and mobius turns. Done on jump skis.

Gates: Space marked by buoys denoting boat path and, in slalom, competitor entry and exit points on the course.

Graphite fiber: A man-made fiber that gives a ski resistance against flex and vibration. It is black in color, very brittle, and looks like hair.

Hit it: Audible signal used by skier to indicate to driver that he is ready for takeoff.

Hole: Towboat moving from resting to planing position is described as "getting out of the hole," or pulling the skier "out of the hole."

Hotdogging: The type of skiing done on large, slalom-type skis, seen on local lakes, includes wake jumps and helicopter flips.

Jacket: A flotation vest worn by all tournament skiers except in the tricks event. *See* PFD.

Jumping: One of the three competitive events in water ski competition. Also an event in barefoot tournaments.

Kevlar: A product trademarked by DuPont, Kevlar is a very expensive, very strong material used in many things, from bullet-proof vests and America's Cup sails to water skis because of its high tensile strength. It's slick and yellow.

Late: Description of a slalom skier who has fallen behind in his rhythmic race through the slalom course. Also used to describe the timing of a jumper's cut toward the ramp.

Leverage: To lean one's body away from the boat, especially in slalom skiing, as if playing tug-of-war against the boat.

Lift: Degree of height gained by a jumper off the ramp.

Line: The tow rope used by a skier. Also used to denote boat path.

Line off: A shortening of the slalom skier's line from the original 75-foot length.

Loop: A splice in a slalom line used in shortening it for line-off runs.

Master board: A plotting board used by tournament officials to determine jump distances by triangulation based on information supplied by meter readers at three sighting stations. Master board is now being replaced in some tournaments with computer programs.

Meters: Stations from which angles of jump landings are sighted. Information furnished to the operator of the master board is used in computing jump distances. Term is also used to describe the sighting arms and angle graphs used at the station.

Narrow: Term used to describe a slalom skier's position in relation to a buoy; generally not far enough outside the line of the buoy. Opposite of wide on a buoy.

Pass: A run through the course as in slalom or tricks. Also used to describe a balk.

PAWS: Professional Association of Waterskiers. Association for professional members of the sport that aids in making rules for competition, and assists promoters.

PFD: Personal Flotation Device. Coast Guard–approved flotation devices for individuals; may be in the form of vests or, in some cases, wetsuits with flotation built in.

Plane: The flat-riding attitude of a boat or ski.

Plate binding: Binding mounted on metal or plastic base that is attached to the ski. Usually used for jumping skis.

Polyprop: Term used to describe the type of olefin material, polypropylene, now used in most water-ski towlines.

Polyurethane foam core: A very high density, two-part foam that's molded to the shape of a ski. Tunnel or concave bottom shapes and bevels are molded into the foam core.

Pop: The act of springing off the wake in jumping or tricks. *See also* Spring.

Pull: The act of accelerating through the wakes of the boat. *See* leverage.

Pylon: A ski tow hitch usually mounted near the boat's center of gravity to compensate for the angular pull of slalom skiers and jumpers.

Quick release: Safety device attached to the towline at the pylon to permit an occupant of the boat to disengage the line when a skier falls. It's commonly used in tricks and may be called a trick release.

Ramp: Takeoff platform used by jumpers.

Rating: The degree of skill attained by a skier and certified by the governing body. AWSA ratings include Novice, Third Class, Second Class, First Class, Expert, and Master.

Reride: A privilege given a skier to repeat a pass if the judges agree an unfair condition existed, such as boat speed out of high tolerance, rough water, etc. Some circumstances, such as low boat speed, make a reride mandatory.

Reverse: Trick performed spinning in the opposite direction. Must be done immediately following a basic spin in order to be calculated as a reverse.

Rideout buoys: In jumping, markers indicating points on the course that a competitor must pass in control of his skis in order for the performance to be scored.

RIM: Reaction injection molded. RIM skis are composed of a polyurethane body with an integral skin, steel or fiberglass rods running lengthwise inside the foam body, and a laminate or aluminum top.

The first step in making a RIM ski is to assemble the reinforcing rods. They are put together with plastic clips that hold them roughly in the shape of a ski. This is placed in the mold. The top of the ski is placed over the top of the mold, and the mold is closed. Material is inserted through a port in the tail of the ski, like filling a doughnut with jelly. After a few minutes the ski is removed from the mold and the excess top skin is trimmed and the ski is finished.

The RIM ski is less expensive than a compression-molded ski, which includes a step of hand-layered fiberglass.

Rocker: The overall bend in the ski downward, from tip to tail.

Rollers: Water condition caused by a boat wake or wind conditions. *See* Backwash.

Rudder: *See* Fin.

Sanction: Approval given by the governing body for a competitive event to take place under conditions specified.

Scorer: Tournament official appointed to maintain the official results of water ski competition.

Side curtain: Safety side of a jump ramp. *See* Apron.

Side slide: A basic maneuver in trick skiing in which the skier moves behind the boat with ski or skis at right angles to his forward progress. Maneuver frequently used by trick skiers on approach to the course to set their desired boat speed.

Slalom: The act of skiing through a course of buoys behind a boat moving at a predetermined speed. One of the three competitive events. Also the single ski used in slalom skiing.

Spring: The act of straightening the legs against the G-force on the jump ramp at the moment of takeoff. The opposite of crush. *See also* Lift; Pop.

Starts, start methods: One of the four events in tournament barefoot skiing.

Stepover: A maneuver in tricks in which the skier steps over the line with his ski or free foot (if on a single ski) while making a 180-, 360-, or 540-degree turn.

Stick skiers: Term used by barefoot skiers to describe traditional skiers.

Third buoy time: Incremental time for the first three buoys in the slalom course; used in competition.

Timer: Tournament official with stopwatch or similar timing device, situated in boat or on shore, to ensure that the boat speed is in tolerance, or that a skier's run in tricks is within the allotted time.

Toehold: An attachment to the trick handle (*see* Bear Trap) for use in toehold maneuvers.

Toe turns: Tricks accomplished with one foot in the handle attachment (toehold).

Tow bar: *See* Hitch; Pylon. Also called a ski handle.

Tricks: The "ballet" of competitive water skiing, consisting of turnarounds, stepovers, somersaults, and other maneuvers described in the official rules. Also individual maneuvers comprising the trick run or one of four competitive events in barefoot competition.

Tune: To alter edges or bottom configuration of a trick ski to enhance its performance.

Tunnel: A more exaggerated concave bottom configuration of a slalom ski.

Unidirectional glass: Small bundles of glass fibers that run from the tip to the tail of the ski. This material helps stiffen the ski and adds weight.

Wake: Disturbed water condition aft caused by forward motion of a towboat. The less disturbance or wave motion, the better for slalom and jumping. Trick skiing requires a pronounced wake table or platform formed by wakes on either side when the boat is operated at slow speeds.

Wax: A special compound used on the surface of a jump ramp and watered down to provide a slick surface for jumper takeoffs.

Wide: A term used to describe where a skier is in relation to the slalom buoy. Opposite of narrow on a buoy.

Wing: An attachment to the fin of a ski that assists the ski in slowing down. Comparable to a "winged keel" on an America's Cup boat, except the wing on a water ski fin is adjustable to different angles.

WWSU: World Water Ski Union. Governing body for organized water skiing worldwide and sanctioning body for the biennial World Water Ski Championships.

Yoke: A rope or semicircular metal rod device attached at either side of a boat transom to serve as a ski hitch. Rope is usually attached to a yoke with a pulley to permit change in direction of pull when a skier makes a turn.

Camille Duvall: Career Highlights

Five-time World Professional Women's Slalom Champion	(1984–85–86–87–88)
Three-time Women's Leading Money Winner of the Coors Light Water Ski Tour	(1984–85–86)
Women's World Slalom Champion	(1985–86 World Championships)
U.S. Masters Women's Slalom Champion	(1984, 1986–87)
U.S. Masters Women's Jumping Champion	(1983)
Tournament of Champions Slalom Champion	(1983–84–85–86–87–88)
Coleman International Slalom Champion	(1988)
Fort Worth Star-Telegram/Long John Silver's Slalom Champion	(1988)
Syracuse Slalom Champion	(1988)
* Budget Rent a Car Orlando Cup Slalom Champion	(1986–87)
* Budget Rent a Car Orlando Cup Jumping Champion	(1987)
Augusta International Slalom Champion	(1986–87)
MasterCraft Invitational Overall Champion	(1987)
Marine World-Coors International Slalom Champion	(1987–88)
Knoxville Classic Slalom Champion	(1987)
Felpausch International Slalom Champion (Detroit, MI)	(1987)
Blazers Classic Jumping Champion (London, England)	(1987)
Oklahoma City International Jumping Champion	(1987)
Wichita International Hydro Cup Slalom Champion	(1986)
Houston-TerraMare Slalom Champion	(1986)

Iron Man Classic Slalom Champion (Birmingham, AL)	(1984–85)
Atlanta International Slalom Champion	(1984–85)
Dayton Hydrobowl Slalom Champion	(1985)
Indianapolis International Slalom Champion	(1985)
Superstars Slalom Champion (Orlando, FL)	(1982–83–84)
Austin Aqua-Fest Slalom Champion	(1984)

Winner of 13 U.S. National titles, including:

U.S. Open Women's Overall Champion	(1977)
U.S. Girls' Overall Champion	(1973–74–75–76)
U.S. Women's Slalom Champion	(1985)
U.S. Girls' Slalom Champion	(1974–75–76)
U.S. Girls' Jumping Champion	(1973, 1976)
U.S. Girls' Tricks Champion	(1973, 1975)

Member of the undefeated world champion U.S. Water Ski Team (1975 to 1978; 1983 to 1987)

Former holder of the "Triple Crown" of Women's Slalom
1985 U.S. National Slalom Champion
1985–86 World Slalom Champion
1986 U.S. Masters Slalom Champion

First female water skier honored by the Women's Sports Foundation (1985–86–87)

Nominated in 1986 and 1987 for the Professional Sportswoman of the Year by the WSF voting members

First female water skier nominated by the U.S. Sports Academy for its version of the Professional Sportswoman of the Year (1986)

Organizer and President of the Athlete's Advisory Council. It marks the first time that male and female professional water skiers have been organized as a group—in 1989, the Council became the Professional Association of Waterskiers (PAWS)

PERSONAL BESTS

Slalom:	3¼ buoys at 38 feet off standard rope line
	Set at 1986 Tournament of Champions
	Coors Light Water Ski Tour Record
Jumping:	148 feet
	Set at the 1987 Houston-TerraMare Classic
Tricks:	5,790 points
	Set at 1985 U.S. Team Trials

* First double-event win, male or female, on the pro tour.